Irene,

Enjoy the read!

Richard John Albero

August 31, 2019

Enjoy the read!

# NOT JUST A
# WALK IN
# THE PARK

*A Sixty-Five-Year-Old Man's Twelve-Hundred-Mile Trek from Tampa to the Bronx*

**RICHARD JOHN ALBERO**

ISBN: 978-1-6847-0260-2 (sc)
ISBN: 978-1-6847-0262-6 (hc)
ISBN: 978-1-6847-0261-9 (e)

Library of Congress Control Number: 2019904924

Lulu Publishing Services rev. date: 05/09/2019

NOT JUST A WALK IN THE PARK

A Sixty-Five-Year-Old Man's Twelve-Hundred-Mile Trek
Tampa to the Bronx
Raising $56,000 in Donations
for Wounded Warriors
in Memory of His Nephew
Lost in 9/11

RICHARD JOHN ALBERO

To my mother,
Lucy,
who firmly believed "family is everything"

# *Contents*

Prologue ........................................................................... xi

Chapter 1   Finding My Soul (or Was I Just Crazy?) ...................... 1
Chapter 2   My Yankee List and My Kids! ................................. 6
Chapter 3   Getting a Sponsor (Easy? Wrong!) ......................... 17
Chapter 4   Training ........................................................... 21
Chapter 5   The Journey Begins! ........................................... 24
Chapter 6   The Rifle Lady (Lady, Don't Shoot Me!) ................... 35
Chapter 7   The Yankee Party ............................................... 47
Chapter 8   One Foot Ahead of the Other .............................. 50
Chapter 9   Mikey and Jacksonville ....................................... 54
Chapter 10  Savannah .......................................................... 70
Chapter 11  The Art of Peeing on the Road, Trucks, and Dogs! ..... 79
Chapter 12  Forty-Nine Hills in Virginia! ................................. 100
Chapter 13  Gary ................................................................ 136
Chapter 14  Did I Find My Soul? ............................................ 137

Epilogue ......................................................................... 141
About the Author ............................................................. 145

# Prologue

In the game of *Monopoly*, Go is the starting point. My starting point is 9/11. *Monopoly* is a game, but my story is not. This is a true story about my simple quest to make the world a better place in which to live, taking advantage of an opportunity to let my family know how much I love them.

I was working as a high school teacher when 9/11 occurred. That day, on my way to class, I remember walking through the library. All the TVs in the library were televising breaking news about 9/11. Immediately at first glance, I knew it was horrific. I continued walking to the adjoining computer lab. The TV set in this classroom was surrounded by students and faculty. I heard the announcement that one of the World Trade Center towers had crumpled. I stayed fixated on the TV. Suddenly it hit me that my nephew Gary worked in the city as an insurance broker for Anon Corporation. I was thinking there was no reason for him to be at the World Trade Center. I could not explain the sensation, but at that instant, I knew Gary was there. *Okay*, I said to myself, *it's not that bad. Gary will be safe.* More news was being released. Suddenly my body had a very strange sensation. At that exact moment, don't ask me why, but I knew that my nephew Gary, godfather to my son, Dante, had lost his life.

Ironically, my nephew Andy, Gary's brother, shared the same gut reaction upon hearing the news about 9/11. He had walked out of his Manhattan office to observe all the smoke from the towers. All of a sudden, he felt like someone had kicked him in the stomach. Andy told me he actually bent over. He knew Gary had to be the reason. He called Ari, Gary's wife of four years, and asked about Gary. Ari told him Gary had just called from the towers. He was on one of the upper floors. Gary informed her he was not going to make it out!

Ari later stated, "He liked talking, and he liked people; the job fit him." She also went on to say, "My husband was my best friend; he loved unconditionally. Gary was a super friendly person and, as a result, had many friends. He liked people, sports, and music. I will always remember Gary as a very happy person who wanted to help people. He will be greatly missed, but his spirit lives on in our son and our hearts. Our loss is heaven's gain."

After the phone call with Ari, Andy immediately walked across town to take a ferry to New Jersey, where he and Gary lived. Once he arrived in New Jersey, other ferries were docking at the same time, coming from the financial district. People were covered with debris and asbestos. Andy said, "It was like watching a movie on TV, except I was in this movie!"

The morning of 9/11, Gary had left his will on the kitchen table for his wife, Ari, to sign off on. Gary had intended to drop the signed will off at his attorney's office later in the week. Was this some kind of weird foreboding? A week later, the chief of the Emerson Police came to Gary's home. Ari was informed that Gary's hand was discovered through DNA testing. His wedding ring was still on it. Ari still wears that ring around her neck to this day.

Pat, my sister-in-law, Gary's mother, had this to say about her son. "From the moment he learned to speak, at a very early age, he was hilarious. When I needed to complete a chore, I would have to turn to my 'off' button. When he and his wife purchased their house, he knew everyone in the neighborhood before they moved in. When we moved into a new house when he was still in college, I would go to the local shopkeepers, and they would say, 'You must be Mrs. Albero.' Gary knew and shared with everyone—even my description, I guess. He was a beloved man. But I want to say to the New York Yankees, he was your biggest fan. When I watched the games on Wednesday and Thursday nights, I could see Gary cheering and yelling 'yay!' and celebrating into the night. I hope wherever he is that he got to enjoy some of your greatest moments."

Sometimes I think about Gary and those last few minutes of his life. What were his last thoughts? Was he in pain? Did he know what had happened? I always try to hit the delete button in my mind when having these thoughts. It's just so painful for me. I rationalize it by saying to myself everything happened instantaneously. No pain, and his soul was immediately taken to heaven.

Andy moved into Gary's house to help Ari with her son, Michael, for the next two weeks. Michael was only a year and a half old. Gary's house was located near a train station. Every time the train whistle sounded, Keno, Gary's German shepherd dog, would run to the door expecting to see Gary walk through it. Andy said, "How do you tell a dog that Gary is not coming home?" Eventually when Keno passed away, his ashes were buried with Gary.

***Gary with his son, Michael.***

*Gary with my son, Dante.*

## Chapter 1

# FINDING MY SOUL
# (OR WAS I JUST CRAZY?)

Don't let the fear of striking out hold you back.
—Babe Ruth

Seven years after 9/11, in preparation for retiring from teaching at the secondary level, I attended a seminar by the New York State Teachers Retirement System. The topic of the seminar was "Entering Retirement: What's Next?" I had attended other NYSTRS seminars. Generally speaking, these were all excellent. The moderator asked us to write down ten things we wanted to do upon retirement. He proceeded to collect ideas from the audience. The presenter posted them on a viewing screen in the front of the room. Most of the items suggested by future retirees were similar. A few of these items were travel, rest, pursue a hobby, volunteer for some charitable organizations, clean out the attic and basement, and get rid of their husband or wife—only kidding! The moderator, while looking at the list written on the screen, stated that the majority of retirees would do almost all ten items within the first six months of retirement—if not sooner!

On my particular list were some items that seemed doable. Others seemed to be just pipe dreams: travel, attend spring training baseball games, spend more time with my family, find a worthwhile hobby, continue doing volunteer work, hike to the bottom of the Grand Canyon, and walk across the United States.

A few years earlier I had decided to retire on a good note rather than on my official end date. That last year of my employment in New

York, I coached successful football and softball teams. My classes were reasonable. My students were responsive! Forty-plus years of teaching were enough. I was fortunate throughout my teaching career. My students respected me. I never once had a student tell me to "F---Off." I would always tell my students, whether it was my math class, physics class, or computer class, that the real name of the class was an educational class in life. On the first day of school each year, I would list my goals for my class on the board. My first and most important goal was for each student to learn something helpful about life from me. Hopefully, someday in the future as an adult, parent, grandparent, boss, or whatever, he or she would say, "You know, Albero was right," and be a better person for it.

Shortly thereafter, with my bucket list saved on my computer, I retired and moved to Florida. Not wanting to get bored in retirement, I obtained a position working as an adjunct instructor at a college in Clearwater. After five wonderful years, I decided to really hang up my cleats and retire fully. Maybe the incentive came when one of my students decided to copy test answers from a student sitting next to him. He really did an excellent job, copying not only all the answers from the paper correctly but the student's name as well. You cannot make this stuff up!

Shortly afterward, I started getting restless. I knew it was time for a new chapter in my life. I decided to hike to the bottom of the Grand Canyon. As I stated previously, the Grand Canyon was one of the top ten items on my bucket list. My son, Dante, and my cousin Donald accompanied me.

A little history is in order here. In 1975, my nephew Gary and I had visited the Grand Canyon when he was fourteen years old. I was driving him and his brother, Andy, across the United States of America. It was quite an adventure and maybe a future book in the making! When we arrived at the Grand Canyon, we took a stroll around the rim. Gary was mesmerized. Upon leaving, Gary and I promised each other to return and hike to the bottom of the canyon. Little did I know that this promise would have many ramifications for me in the future.

Gary was a tremendous Yankees fan. One time, he drove from his home in New Jersey to my house in upstate New York so we could attend a night game against the Red Sox at Fenway Park. It was the middle of the week. I decided to drive. Backing out of my garage, I smashed into Gary's car. In my defense, I was not used to having a car parked behind me. Gary walked over to his car, shook his head, and said, "Don't worry about it, Uncle Rich. Let's get to the game!"

At that time, Gary was living in a low-rent district. He became a Big Brother to a boy named Ryan, who lived with his mother on the floor below. Gary dedicated several years to Ryan's upbringing. This included helping him with homework, teaching him how to hit a baseball and run with a football, and instructing him on good manners. Ryan would eventually be in Gary's wedding party. Unfortunately, he would also give a eulogy at Gary's funeral.

Gary was well respected and loved. More than one thousand people were at his funeral service at Saint Andrew's, a very large Catholic church in Westwood, New Jersey. Yet the church still did not have enough room for all the people paying their last respects to this kind, loving, and giving individual.

Gary had a reputation for always being late to family get-togethers. It was so bad that the family would tell him a time an hour earlier than the actual time of the family event. When my son, Dante, was going to be baptized, Gary had been chosen to be the godfather. As the ceremony started, there was no Gary! He was late. Big surprise! My brother, Andy, Gary's father, had to step in and act as a surrogate. Gary eventually showed up with a big grin on his face—a face that you could not stay mad at.

Today every time I visit Gary's son, Michael, I see so many of Gary's features in him. When I leave Michael's house, there are always some tears in my eyes. I never could make sense out of bin Laden's logic. What did he really accomplish? No seventy-two virgins for him—unless they all had the clap! I'm sure God has punished him. I firmly believe hell is not enough punishment for bin Laden.

When my son, my cousin Gerald, and I reached the bottom of the Grand Canyon, we had a little service for Gary. We buried some of his personal items. Together, we said a prayer. Tears were rolling down my cheeks. I felt Gary touching my soul. I somehow knew Gary was going to touch my soul again.

Little did I know how much!

Fast-forwarding, with retirement going well, I was now living in a nice home in Dunedin, Florida, with no attic or basement to clean!

I was volunteering at a food pantry weekly, doing various odds and ends to keep busy. During this time, my older daughter, Lucia, had decided to come and live with me for a year. Always upbeat and optimistic about life, Lucia would soon play a role in my life-changing decision to do something unique: walk from Tampa, Florida, to the Bronx, New York. It would be not just a walk in the park but a walk in honor of my nephew Gary.

My initial thoughts were to walk across the country, similar to the cross-country driving trip I had done with my nephews in 1975. I started doing some extensive research for walking across the United States. About a month after researching and roughing out routes and other logistics, reality set in. I was nuts! I could not afford it or leave my Saint Bernard, Moe, for that amount of time. It would take months to do the walk. And I didn't know who would be my support drivers for that amount of time. I also didn't know about the cost! Maybe being older and now more realistic about things, I knew the trip across the country was not realistic.

Not wanting to give up so easily on my adventurous bucket list, my next planned endeavor was to hike the Appalachian Trail. Undaunted, I again started my research, this time reading books by hikers who had completed the trail. Did I want to spend that much time alone? Once more, my dog was an issue in regard to time. The next and final nail in the coffin was the probability of bears and snakes! To say I have a fear of snakes is putting it mildly. If a snake would surprise me on the trail, I would set the world record for the one hundred meters. On the plus side, I would cut at least a month off my trip. Let's just say that reality set in again. No Appalachian Trail hike for me!

Lucia kept encouraging me, saying that I would find an adventure to sink my teeth in. Most of my friends and family just blew me off about my ideas. In my heart, I knew I would come up with something.

A few days after saying that to myself, I went to visit Steinbrenner Field in Tampa. This is the spring training complex for the New York Yankees. As soon as I entered the complex, I saw a stunning statue of George Steinbrenner. It's a six-hundred-pound, life-size statue on a three-foot-high granite pedestal that is identical to one in the lobby of Yankee Stadium. For nonbaseball folks, George Steinbrenner was the principal owner of the Yankees for thirty-seven years.

George was like everybody else in life. He had his ups and downs.

After reading a few books about George, I basically was of the opinion he was a very charitable and a good man. People who criticize him should heed a phrase my father always said to me: "Don't criticize somebody for doing something until you've walked in his shoes." George was a very frank and charitable person. George had done many benevolent acts for those in need, especially in the Tampa area. So, yes, I was a fan of George. I respected all his kind acts—not to mention saving the Yankees from CBS! Older Yankee fans know exactly what I mean by that statement.

So here I was standing in front of Mr. Steinbrenner's statue admiring the artistry and construction of the statue. Call it an epiphany, a daydream, just being crazy, or whatever. It hit me, I could walk to Yankee Stadium from Steinbrenner field. What could it be, twelve hundred miles? Why would I do it? How would I do it? Come on, Rich, get out of here; George is going to think you're crazy! As I continued to stand there and think about it, ideas just kept shooting through my brain, too many to mention. Was I crazy? Well, I knew the answer to that!

I settled on the following. I would do the walk in honor of my nephew Gary, raise money for a charity, and maybe find out some answers about life, which I would soon be referring to as finding my soul.

# Chapter 2

# MY YANKEE LIST AND MY KIDS!

It isn't a calamity
To die with dreams unfulfilled
But it is a calamity not to dream.
—Benjamin E. Mays

Once I settled in my head that this walk was going to be from Tampa to the Bronx, I started laying the groundwork. Lucia was firmly in my corner. Lucia said constantly that it would be great. She kept encouraging me. Here are some of Lucia's recollections about this time.

> "I'm going to do it," my father exclaimed as he walked through the garage door. "I'm going to do it! I'm going to walk from Tampa to the Bronx!"
>
> "What?" I said, looking up from playing tug-of-war with Moe, our 180-pound Saint Bernard pup.
>
> "Today I was at Steinbrenner Field, checking out some new Yankee gear, and suddenly, I stopped right in front of the statue of George. George stood for greatness, perseverance, dedication, and always being the best version of yourself that you can be. I knew looking up at him today, I have something great to give."
>
> "A walk," he said. "A walk that begins at Steinbrenner Field in Tampa and ends at Yankee Stadium."

"Dad, are you serious? That's a nineteen-hour drive with Dante driving, and you know he only allows us five-minute bathroom breaks! How long is the walk going to take?"

"I'm not sure," he said sturdily. "I believe it's about twelve hundred miles, though, and I want to do it for a charity."

There's one thing I knew about my father: if he sets his mind to something, he is going to do it. "Okay, Dad, well, if you feel this strongly about it, there's a reason for it, and you have to see it to fruition." I knew that if this dream was placed in his heart, there was a bigger purpose for it.

My father has one of the biggest hearts you could ever imagine. Growing up, we always had "sponsored siblings," Bernie from the Philippines and Prince from Costa Rica. Each year we would get cards that said, "Ten chickens have been donated in your honor to provide eggs for families in need." My sister, Felicia, always loved when he donated donkeys in her honor for plowing and planting. He also was involved in Habitat for Humanity, the Alzheimer's Association, and Saint Vincent de Paul, helping give people below the poverty line financial assistance. On Wednesdays he would cook his famous chicken noodle soup for a soup kitchen in Ocala, Florida, and he has also trained our Saint Bernard puppy, Mia, to be a certified therapy dog, going into hospitals and being a furry friend for patients right out of surgery or giving blood. Since this has been my dad's heartfelt character, I knew this walk was right in line with his life's purpose.

During training, *many* people laughed at his dream. "There's no way you're going to make it!" "You're going to get run over by a car!" "Are you doing this because you think this will put hair on your head?" So many people spoke words of defeat about his walk.

I told him, "Dad, if you truly see yourself walking safely from Tampa to the Bronx, connecting people with your heartfelt journey and raising money for a charitable cause, then don't let *anyone* stand in your way. Don't let those negative words take root in your mind. When they come, *delete* them, and fill them with words of victory. I will step on home plate at Yankee Stadium; I will raise over $50,000 for a charitable cause; I will show people how important random acts of kindness are. To be successful on this journey, you first need to believe it, see yourself achieving the goal, and then speak words of victory. Remember your words form your world.

"You're right. I know I have to focus on this goal, believe it, and then achieve it."

And he did. Eighty-eight days later, my dad proudly walked into Yankee Stadium with a group of thankful wounded warriors, triumphantly stepping on home plate, without any injury, having raised $56,000 for veterans and service members who graciously gave their lives for our protection and freedom.

To me, my dad's journey represented hard work, faith, goal setting, being a part of a cause that's greater than you, and showing the world that anything is possible. If there is a dream placed in your heart, there is a reason for it, and you have to see it out to fruition. We all have seeds of greatness inside of us. What's your gift to give?

On the other hand, when I ran my idea by my friends, their support seemed, at best, half-hearted. Their tone seemed to say, "Are you nuts?" I didn't give it a second thought; my mind was made up.

I began the process. Looking back now, I see I was very naïve about all the ramifications of this walk. I was slow to comprehend how dangerous it would be, the enormity of the logistics, and how physically demanding it would be to do the walk. Finally, and probably most critical, was whether or not I had the mental fortitude to accomplish such a grueling undertaking. I was sixty-five years old!

At the same time, I was trying to find a charity to sponsor me. This endeavor was the first of many unforeseen letdowns to come. I began by calling several very notable charities. Foolishly I thought they would jump on the bandwagon to sponsor me in my trip from Tampa to the Bronx. It wasn't until I spoke with a person on the phone from the ALS (amyotrophic lateral sclerosis) Association that reality began to come to light. She told me the hard facts: Most nonprofit organizations were not going to sponsor me. Why? Too much liability—what if I got hit by a car or truck or had some other injury during the walk? They didn't know me from Adam. What would happen if I was some nutcase, a sexual deviant, or worst yet, a Communist? Also, she informed me most nonprofits would only sponsor short-term events. Finally, the bottom line was that nonprofits wanted corporate sponsors!

In the following few weeks, after much time, effort, and several phone calls, I found out the ALS representative's information was very accurate. Undaunted, I put a sponsorship on the back burner and focused my attention on the logistics of the walk. That's when I came up with the mother lode idea. At that time, I didn't realize how unique a concept it was! My creative idea was to name each mile after a present or former Yankee player. People wishing to donate could choose the amount of money to donate and find a corresponding Yankee player and his mile for that amount.

I needed a starting place to obtain my pool of Yankee players. I decided on 1913, when the Yanks started to be called the New York Yankees, rather than 1903 when they started in the American League. At that time, the Yankees did not have an official nickname. They were often called the New York Americans in reference to the American League. Another name given was the Highlanders after a British military unit, the Golden Highlanders.

Now having a starting point (1913), I began listing the players. Little did I know how many hours it would take to establish a complete accurate list. Eventually I grouped the players into six categories—designated hitter, single, double, triple, home run, and grand slam. For nonbaseball readers, a designated hitter is a player who only hits and doesn't play defense. A grand slam is a home run with runners on first base, second base, and third base.

I decided to list every Yankee player who wore the uniform, even if for only one game. Being a type A personality, I wanted the list to be as accurate as possible. In the back of my mind, I was sure somebody would contact me during my walk, telling me about a Yankee player I forgot or some other criticism. There's always the geeks and the (you fill in the blank).

After many hours and weeks of research on the internet, trips to the library, and purchasing several books on the Yankees, I completed my list. It was a total of 1,649 players. Included were some managers—namely, Casey Stengel, Miller Huggins, John McGraw, Bucky Harris, Joe Torre, and owner George Steinbrenner, whom I added to my master list.

I had estimated my trip would be approximately twelve hundred miles. I assigned a Yankee player to each mile. Each player was placed into one of the following categories: walk, single, double, triple, home run, or grand slam and each category had a suggested donation attached. With more Yankee players than miles to walk, the extra players were inserted into the designated hitter category, where a five-dollar donation was recommended.

From the get-go, I was somewhat prejudiced toward certain Yankees, both in a positive and negative way. So my list definitely differed from those posted on the internet and other places that listed the top ten or top hundred Yankee players. The last nine miles of my walk were dedicated to the home run category. The grand slam category had just one player.

This last and most highly rated mile (walking into Yankee Stadium) was named after the one and only *Babe Ruth*. Babe Ruth in my mind was and always will be the greatest player of all time. Plus he had the face of an angel! Here are a few of Babe's achievements:

- first in all-time slugging percentage, OPS, and OPS+
- second in on-base percentage, all-time RBI list
- third in all-time home run list, bases on balls

- seven-time World Series champion
- 1923 MVP
- six-time AL RBI champion, AL batting champion (1916), twelve-time AL home run champion
- Major League Baseball All-Century team
- member of Hall of Fame

I have several memorabilia items of the Babe—including a cookie jar and several pictures of him in and out of uniform. Also, many baseball cards and God only knows how many T-shirts with his picture. One of my cherished pictures of him is playing bocce. I even have one of his replica cigars! Also, I have several watches with his image on them.

On his birthday, every February 6, while teaching class, I would always wear one of the watches with a picture of his face on the watch. During the class, I would hit a certain button on the watch. It would play "Take Me Out to the Ballgame." My students loved it!

There is no limit to the number of books, movies, and testimonies to the Babe that exist—there are just too many for me to mention here. But in this book, my book, on this earth, he was the god of baseball.

A $1,000 donation was the suggested dollar amount set as a minimum for any of the last ten miles walking to Yankee Stadium. Here is a list of my top ten players:

1. George Herman "Babe" Ruth—"The Bambino"
2. Lou Gehrig—"The Iron Horse"
3. Mickey Charles Mantle—"The Commerce Comet"
4. Lawrence Peter Berra—"Yogi"
5. Derek Jeter—"The Captain"
6. Mariano Rivera—"Mo"
7. Edward Charles "Whitey" Ford—"The Chairman of the Board"
8. George Steinbrenner—"The Boss"
9. Joseph Paul DiMaggio—"The Yankee Clipper"
10. Casey Stengel—"The Old Professor"

A minimum donation of $1,000 was recommended for any of these players. Remember these were the last ten miles walking into

Yankee Stadium. This might sound selfish, but in my mind, I was doing the walk. Therefore, I could put them in any kind of ranking as I wished. Having said that, I apologize for any other Yankee you would have wanted to put in the top ten. If you're upset with me, that's okay. Keep your anger down. Wait till you read my top one hundred (triple category)! I really inserted my personal bias there.

A $500 donation was the dollar amount set as a minimum for any of the hundred players in the group designated as triples:

| | | | |
|---|---|---|---|
| 1. | Elston Howard | 30. | Johnny Sain |
| 2. | Thurman Munson | 31. | Joe Dugan |
| 3. | Don Mattingly | 32. | Joe Gordon |
| 4. | Roger Maris | 33. | Joe Collins |
| 5. | Bill Dickey | 34. | Red Rolfe |
| 6. | Tony Lazzeri | 35. | Luis Arroyo |
| 7. | Ed Lopat | 36. | Jerry Coleman |
| 8. | Jack Chesbro | 37. | Alfonso Soriano |
| 9. | David Winfield | 38. | Willie Randolph |
| 10. | Phil Rizzuto | 39. | Bernie Williams |
| 11. | Goose Gossage | 40. | Sparky Lyle |
| 12. | Frank Chance | 41. | Tommy Henrich |
| 13. | Earle Combs | 42. | Mel Stottlemyre |
| 14. | Lefty Gomez | 43. | Ron Guidry |
| 15. | Burleigh Grimes | 44. | Jorge Posada |
| 16. | Waite Hoyt | 45. | Roy White |
| 17. | Willie Keeler | 46. | Ed Figueroa |
| 18. | Johnny Mize | 47. | Chris Chambliss |
| 19. | Herb Pennock | 48. | Lou Piniella |
| 20. | Joe Sewell | 49. | Paul O'Neill |
| 21. | Red Ruffing | 50. | Spud Chandler |
| 22. | Enos Slaughter | 51. | Hank Bauer |
| 23. | Dazzy Vance | 52. | Charlie Keller |
| 24. | Paul Waner | 53. | Dave Righetti |
| 25. | Catfish Hunter | 54. | Bobby Richardson |
| 26. | Wade Boggs | 55. | Bill Skowron |
| 27. | Stan Coveleski | 56. | Ralph Terry |
| 28. | Rickey Henderson | 57. | Allie Reynolds |
| 29. | Home Run Baker | 58. | Frank Crosetti |

59. Vic Raschi
60. Tino Martinez
61. Bobby Murcer
62. David Cone
63. Al Downing
64. Snuffy Stirnweiss
65. Clete Boyer
66. Bucky Dent
67. Hideki Matsui
68. Bob Meusel
69. Hal Chase
70. Graig Nettles
71. Sal Maglie
72. Tommy John
73. Tom Tresh
74. Bob Shawkey
75. Mike Mussina
76. George Selkirk
77. Jim Kaat
78. Gil McDougald
79. Tony Kubek

80. Ryne Duren
81. Tommy Byrne
82. Bobby Brown
83. Mickey Rivers
84. Bobby Shantz
85. Billy Martin
86. Joe Page
87. Johnny Murphy
88. Monte Pearson
89. George Pipgras
90. Joe Pepitone
91. Gene Woodling
92. Don Larsen
93. Joe Torre—Manager
94. John McGraw—Manager
95. Bucky Harris—Manager
96. Miller Huggins—Manager
97. Joe McCarthy—Manager
98. Ben Chapman
99. Bill McKechnie
100. Reggie Jackson

My next list comprised 490 Yankee players. These players made up the doubles category. A one-hundred-dollar donation was the amount set as a minimum for this category. The next category was singles, which required a donation of fifty dollars and consisted of three hundred players. The next grouping was walks, which was a donation of twenty-five dollars and consisted of three hundred players. Finally, for a five-dollar donation, there was the designated hitters list consisting of 449 players.

As I continued to sort out my list, I was working part-time as an adjunct instructor at a local college in Clearwater, Florida. In the fall of 2015, I announced to my class it would be my last semester teaching. I informed them about my proposed walk from Tampa to the Bronx. When I was finished talking, they all started clapping for me. I was really moved and taken aback. Thankfully, I had established a good rapport with them.

I felt they were telling me, "We know you can do it, we trust you

Mr. A, and you're cool!" Or maybe a few students in the back of the classroom were saying, "Thank God he's leaving!" Maybe it's a coincidence or the powers above, but as I'm writing this draft, I received a text message from a former student, whom I taught approximately ten years ago.

> Good morning, Professor Albero. Today is National Teacher Appreciation Day. Therefore, I wanted you to know that it was a blessing and privilege to have taken your class. Thank you for what you've done. Your favorite student *ever*!

With my students' support and reinforcement from my son, Dante, and my daughters, Lucia and Felicia, I continued working on my Yankee list. It was really motivating to me to see how much blind faith my children had in their sixty-five-year-old father. Maybe this was earned from all the hard work being a single parent. I did most of their parenting as they grew up.

Thinking back on those days, several memorable and heartwarming events come to mind. One time when I visited my daughter Lucia in her senior year at college in Albany, we went out for dinner at a local restaurant. As we were sitting at the bar having a drink, waiting for our table, she glanced at me and said, "You know, Dad, I look at you not only as a father now, but as a human being with feelings and emotions." Lucia went on to explain not only how much respect she had for me as a single parent but also as a caring individual. I kidded her, saying it only took twenty-one years for her to realize it. It made me feel very warm and humble inside.

Lucia and I shared many touching moments together. She was my partner at several volunteer functions I did over the years. We served together at a Thanksgiving food kitchen. I volunteered at an overnight shelter for several years. Lucia joined me several times at this shelter. We cooked many volunteer dinners together for the homeless. We had many laughs about trying to get the rickety old stove to work correctly to make those dinners.

Another of my favorite memories with Lucia is Christmas Eve when she was a junior in high school. We were driving through Poughkeepsie, New York, giving out small gifts I had wrapped for the homeless. It was fairly late at night. We were definitely not in the very best section of town. I could see she was getting nervous when I stopped the Jeep and had her hand out gifts to the homeless people. By the expression on her face, I could tell Lucia was getting scared. I said to her, "How can you be scared? We have Moe (our pet dog) in the back of the car." Moe literally adored her and would protect her from anything. Oh, did I mention that Moe was a 180-pound Saint Bernard? Lucia turned her head and looked at Moe smiling and drooling in the back seat. She just started to laugh.

*Moe.*

My younger daughter, Felicia, had her moments with me as well. One day when I was taking a nap, Felicia came running into my room. She had her prom dress in her hand. She was so excited, shouting at me, jumping up and down while showing me her prom dress. I just thought to myself how lucky I was to have such a beautiful daughter.

Of course, there were other moments. Such as when I had to attend her cheerleading contests. I had to be there for the start, at eight in the morning, sit in the bleachers (very uncomfortable!) with all the mothers, and hope the competition would end before eight in the evening.

Finally, Friday nights were another story. Felicia would always have at least four, if not eight, of her friends spending the night. Most of the parents of these girls knew my character and had no issue with their daughters sleeping over. It was a tiny home, less than a thousand square feet. My bedroom was located out on the sunporch. The teenage girls loved asking me questions they felt uncomfortable asking their own parents. Sometimes I wished they asked different questions. Being a high school teacher and coach, I had experienced many situations with young adolescents. It was the best thing about teaching. It kept you young.

Once, when doing a training walk with my son in Dunedin, Dante started opening up to me about the ramifications of having divorced parents. During the conversation, he told me one of the things he remembered most about me. I thought maybe it was when I was coaching his Little League team, Babe Ruth team, or high school football team or taking him to see the Yankee World Series Parade in New York City. To my surprise and delight, none of these were his answer. His response gave my soul and heart a shake!

When he was younger, I would walk up to his bus stop every day to pick him up at the end of the day. One morning I had a very bad car accident; my car even caught on fire. I had a lot of bruises and was literally knocked out from hitting my head on the front windshield. Thank God I have a hard head, but my car was totaled. Dante said he would never forget me limping up to the bus stop to pick him up that same afternoon from school. I had no idea that was one of the most impressible memories he had of me. It brought tears to my eyes and rocked my soul. In an odd way, as an upshot of his revelation, I knew the roots of determination were starting to swell within me to do this walk!

*Chapter 3*

# GETTING A SPONSOR
# (EASY? WRONG!)

A humble knowledge of oneself is a surer road to God.
—Unknown

After completing my Yankee lists, the next most important step was again trying to secure a sponsor. After numerous attempts, I had received rejections for various or no reasons at all why they could not sponsor me. My depression was escalating again. I knew it was a great concept. Yet nobody wanted me! In spite of these setbacks, my daughter Lucia continued her undaunted support by declaring, "Don't worry, Dad. Something will happen. This is a great idea."

The next day I came across the Wounded Warrior Project web page. After researching them and being a retired reserve naval officer, I felt they might be a fit. After several calls and another couple of weeks passing by, the Wounded Warrior Project gave me the go-ahead to register my walk with them. They would gladly accept any donations from my walk. They wished me luck. Like the song, "I was so excited." Unfortunately, that feeling became short-lived when they subsequently informed me of their stipulations. They would sponsor me and list me on their web page as an event; however, they instructed me to just send the donations I collected to the Wounded Warrior Project when my event ended. I didn't know if it was because they were such a large entity or they thought I was a nutcase. Whatever their reason, basically they were only willing to accept any money I received and, at this time, not give any type of real support.

Undaunted, I set up a meeting with a Wounded Warrior representative in Tampa. I chatted with him about my concept. I asked if he could give me a couple of shirts, hats, or a rain jacket with the Wounded Warrior Project logo to wear on my trip. His response was that they had to buy their own stuff. He might get me a discount! After the meeting, I walked out. I cannot put in print what I was thinking to myself.

Essentially, I was offering to walk from Tampa, Florida, to Bronx, New York, and raise money for their organization. Yet I couldn't even get a hat or shirt from them! In their defense, they sent me some plastic bracelets and small magnets with the Wounded Warrior Project logo! Talk about feeling dejected! The Wounded Warrior Project did make amends later on.

At this point I was resigned to doing the walk unsponsored. Even if I only raised two dollars, it would be worth doing for Gary's memory. Thinking that I had hit rock bottom—wrong (rock bottom was still to come!)—I made up some banners and a sign detailing my proposed walk for the Wounded Warrior Project.

I went to a CrossFit gym in Saint Petersburg owned by one of my daughter's friends. I set up a table with information flyers of my walk. I had my plastic bracelets with me. Well, people loved getting the free Wounded Warrior Project bracelets! Total donations after eight hours—twenty-five dollars: a long way from the goal of $25,000 that I had set in my head.

Still, I was not totally discouraged, but I recognized I had a huge hole to fill. I had been envisioning my sponsor covering all my expenses, supplying public relations, maybe even a dedicated PR person, and so on. Boy, this was a rude awakening. Without the encouragement of my daughter Lucia, I might have given up right then.

Again, Lucia's support motivated me to devote many hours to researching and follow up with major contributors to the Wounded Warrior Project. Online, I came across a list of Hollywood actors and directors who had previously sponsored Wounded Warrior Project events. I wrote out over a hundred letters (no kidding) to them and other possible sponsors to assist me with financial support or donate equipment for my walk. This list included, to name a few, a famous portable camera company, various sneaker companies, sport apparel companies, books-on-tape companies, a major sport ID bracelet company, and sport water companies.

Notice I did not mention any names. The purpose of this book is not to embarrass any company or person. Although to be candid, I do feel some of them really didn't care. Some of the companies and individuals responded. I am forever thankful for their courtesy of a response.

But it wasn't all negative. I did get my first corporate donation. A company not even from the United States! It was the Tilley Company, based in Toronto, Canada. They donated a hat and several pairs of socks to me. How ironic that my first contribution was from a company outside the United States. I will always be indebted to the Tilley Company. I will always have a place in my heart for them. They were the first to receive a thank you letter from me. Getting that support from the Tilley Company was just enough encouragement to keep me from hitting rock bottom and chucking my walk down the drain. God bless the Canadians! If this book ever gets printed, I'm sending the Tilley Company one of the first books off the press!

Another bout of despair, just one donation, and it was not even from my country! Without support money, there was no way I could pull this off. I had been so wrapped up in this phase, I never gave a thought to some other very pertinent items. For example, whether I could do the walk, would it be dangerous, and what kind of logistics would be needed? I didn't know whether this was self-confidence or just a strong belief in God, but I never considered any of these issues as being a problem. Wouldn't my teachers (nuns) from elementary school be proud of that statement!

One day while still working on my list and trying to get out of my depression, I received a phone call from Robert Michaels, an orthopedic doctor living on Long Island. He informed me he was involved with a midget football team from Roslyn. Roslyn is a community in Long Island, New York. Their youth football league raised money every year for a charitable organization. Robert Michaels had called the Wounded Warrior Project to see about making a donation to them. The Wounded Warrior Project said great, just send us the check! He wanted his young football players to see how much benefit their donation was making. After all, they had worked very hard raising this money to donate. They didn't just want to send a check in the mail.

Upon further research of the Wounded Warrior Project home page, Robert came across my name. He then decided to reach out to me by phone. In our phone conversation, I told him how I was planning on walking from Tampa, Florida, to the Bronx, New York, in honor of my nephew Gary, who was a victim of 9/11. Also, I informed him that each mile of the walk would be named after a Yankee player. We talked and talked. At the end of the phone conversation, Robert told me he would donate the football team's money to my Wounded Warrior project. Also, Robert said he had a good friend named Andrew Levy, who had many contacts with the Yankees. His business was in sports marketing. Robert told me Andrew might be able to give me some direction. He proceeded to give me Andrew Levy's number.

That same day I gave Andrew a call. We talked for quite a bit. I think Andrew thought I was a little nuts. But somehow he was receiving a vibe I was a good man. I was getting the same vibe from him as well. He didn't mention any type of fee for his services. He said he would check things out and get back to me. Little did I know at this time, he would be my lifesaver and a future lifelong friend.

*Chapter 4*

# TRAINING

You can't turn back the clock.
But you can wind it up again.
—Bonnie Prudden

People always ask me how much training I did before starting my walk. Actually, I did not do a lot. My premise was if I went into a hard-core training routine at age sixty-five, something would break down. Then my walk would only be a dream. Having said this, I did realize my feet would have to be toughened up. I wasn't looking to set any speed records. When doing calculations for the walk, ninety days looked pretty realistic to me. If I averaged fifteen-plus miles a day, the walk would be doable. So my goal was to work up to fifteen miles a day by the time I started the trip and add mileage as the walk went on.

Believe it not, my initial training started with two-mile walks. When I started my walk, my daughter Lucia always said to the reporters I went out to get the mail one day and just never returned! Looking back on my training walks, I remember taking breaks after five miles, taking my sneakers off, putting first aid cream on my blisters. I would massage my feet. While rubbing my feet, I kept thinking to myself, "Are you freaking nuts about actually doing this walk?" Well, the blisters did lessen, but my head games got worse. This walk just seemed like a silly thought. Each day reality set in more and more. Eventually I walked up to twenty-one miles in one day. This was a major accomplishment. However, boredom was another real issue to deal with. I didn't really have a remedy for this boredom problem except listening to my music and books on tape.

Eventually my thought process started to change a little. I could do this walk. I never thought about all the ramifications, the cost, what if I got hurt, or what if I quit! Maybe I was just at a stage in my life becoming bored and just needing something. The training, if you want to call it that, was just something to do. But somewhere down deep, my soul kept gnawing at me, saying, "You're all in on this."

At this stage, if it was a poker hand, I didn't even have a pair of deuces or anything close to a good hand to be able to stay in the game. Looking back now, I always felt like things would work out. I would find a way to overlook any adversity. Maybe it was cockiness, determination, or just faith, but this walk was somehow becoming a reality to me. I wasn't scared or intimidated—maybe just naïve.

When not walking, my days were filled compiling and organizing the list of Yankee players, writing letters, soliciting donations, designing Excel sheets to do financial projections for the walk. At this time, I never really gave much thought to walking routes or who were going to be my support drivers. As a former physics teacher, I recognized that the ball was rolling and picking up momentum. Could I deal with all the friction factors, especially the discouragement factor with not getting sponsors at this point in time?

In the meantime, Andrew Levy, through his Wish You Were Here Productions company, had contacted representatives in the Yankee organization about my walk.

Soon afterward, I received a call from Jason Zillo, Yankees PR director, and Brian Cashman, Yankees General Manager. They told me how they never in all their years with the Yankees had anyone come up with a concept like mine, naming each mile after a New York Yankee player for a fund-raiser. What a great concept! I was proud as a peacock. They were very excited for me. Both of them gave me some valuable advice. The most important suggestion was to have a separate phone contact. At that moment, little did I know what a foreshadowing this would be. Phone calls both out and incoming would be one of the more difficult tasks I would encounter on my adventure.

The Yankees called to set up an interview with me at my house. They sent out a crew from YES (Yankees Entertainment and Sports Network). My daughter Lucia was so excited for me. She kept saying to me, "See, I told you things were going to work out. All your work and effort are going to pay off!"

The New York Yankees sports channel was coming to my house. I couldn't believe it. Was I dreaming? If nothing else, it gave me an excuse to clean my house! It was kind of surreal when they arrived. Things were happening so fast, it was like a dream. Yet reality was setting in. However, I was so locked into the logistics of the walk, I had no time to think about how hard and dangerous the walk was going to be. This was definitely a good thing!

The full interview can be seen on the following website: https://www.youtube.com/watch?v=7sbIguvLphY.

*Chapter 5*

# THE JOURNEY BEGINS!

People may doubt what we say,
But they'll believe what we do.
—Lewis Cass

March 2, 2015, arrived—the first day of my walk. The drive over to Steinbrenner Field from my home in Dunedin was relatively calm. I was just taking one minute at a time. I still had not given much thought to the totality of this walk. What kind of difficulties might arise? Maybe I was being naïve, or maybe it was just my way of keeping positive. Excluding my three children and my football coach/teacher from high school, I remember thinking no one really thought I could do this nutty walk. The coach, Bill, was going to be one of my support drivers. Eventually Bill would be one of the main reasons I would complete my walk. My children just had blind faith in me.

It didn't really bother me that nobody believed I could complete the walk or I was seriously attempting to do it. I just had a quiet confidence in myself and a trust in God that I would do it.

Before arriving at Steinbrenner Field, I was accompanied by my friend Jimmy and my son, Dante. We stopped at a local restaurant for breakfast in Tampa. I was wearing my walking shirt with this saying on the front: "Walking from Tampa to the Bronx."

A man approached our table while we were eating breakfast. He asked, "Are you the guy walking from Tampa to the Bronx?"

I looked down at my shirt and said, "Yes!"

He asked if he could get a picture with me. He informed us he saw a news report on TV the night before about me.

I said, "Sure." This was going to be fun; I was becoming a star! Little did I know there was going to be a price for this fleeting moment of stardom.

*My walking shirt.*

A short time after breakfast, Dante and I drove over to Steinbrenner Field. The night before was pretty uneventful. My premise was that the less I thought about the walk, the less there was to worry about.

As we arrived at Steinbrenner Field, a lot of local reporters were standing in the parking lot waiting to interview me. My son was wearing his Yankee jersey. As we exited the car, Dante was immediately grabbed by a reporter for an interview. I felt so happy for him. I watched him chat with a reporter and listened to his responses. One of Dante's remarks to the reporter was, "He's crazy, but when he sets his mind to something, he can do it." Another comment was, "I don't know if I could do it. Here I am twenty-six, and my sixty-five-year-old father is about to make this trek of twelve hundred miles. Couldn't be happier for him." I was so very proud of him. At that moment I was not thinking about my walk, but about how much I love my son.

My brother Michael and his wife, Paula, my sister Rose Ann, my sister-in-law Deborah, and my good friend Jimmy accompanied me through security into the stadium.

I have known Jimmy since I was four years old. He was going to be my first support driver. A couple of days prior at my home in Dunedin, Jimmy in a delicate way was trying to hint he wanted to say something to me.

I said, "Jimmy, what's up?"

Jimmy, in his own kind way, told me I was not going to be able to complete this walk. I was sixty-five years old, and my knees probably would not hold up or something else would break down. Basically, he said my walk was not realistic. It's kind of funny now, since here I am at this moment writing this book.

Jimmy recently was at my home for a visit. We were chatting.

Out of the blue, he told me that he couldn't believe I did the walk. "You, Rich, walked from Tampa to the Bronx; what a great feat it was." I felt very proud. His comments made me feel really good for a lot of different reasons. It gave me validation to what I had accomplished. A fellow peer, not prone to giving praise, and a respected friend was complimenting me!

# New York Yankees
## —————— OFFICIAL PRESS RELEASE

Yankee Stadium • One East 161st Street, Bronx, NY • Phone: (718) 579-4460 • E-mail: media@yankees.com

FEBRUARY 28, 2015

### RETIRED TEACHER TO WALK 1,200 MILES
### FROM HOME PLATE AT STEINBRENNER FIELD IN TAMPA TO HOME PLATE
### AT YANKEE STADIUM IN THE BRONX IN SUPPORT OF THE WOUNDED WARRIOR PROJECT

On Monday, March 2, at 10:00 a.m., **Richard J. Albero**, a formal naval officer and educational professional, will begin a walk from home plate at Steinbrenner Field in Tampa, Fla., to home plate at Yankee Stadium in the Bronx, N.Y., — a trek over 1,200 miles — in support of the Wounded Warrior Project.

To honor his nephew Gary Albero, who died in the 9/11 attacks, Mr. Albero wanted to raise money for the Wounded Warrior Project, while incorporating Gary's love for the New York Yankees. To do this, each mile of the walk is dedicated to a different New York Yankees player in the team's history.

Mr. Albero's intent is to raise $25,000 for the Wounded Warrior Project, with $9,000 already having been reached. Donations may be made in the form of "Designated Hitter," "Base on Balls," "Single," "Double," "Triple," "Home Run" or "Grand Slam."

"My goal is to support the soldiers who have bravely fought to protect us," said Mr. Albero.

Walking an average of 20 miles a day, the 65-year-old Mr. Albero plans to complete the journey within three months with support drivers by his side.

To make a donation, please go to **richardsyankeeswalk.org**.

Media needing a daily credential for covering his departure from Steinbrenner Field should submit their request via e-mail to credentials@yankees.com. Questions may be directed to that e-mail address or to Yankees Media Relations representative Alexandra Trochanowski at (813) 673-3053.

*New York Yankees Press Release.*

I and my entourage (I was upgrading my vocabulary now that my fame was growing! Seriously, things were happening so fast now. I did not have time to get a big head.) were escorted into the Yankees dugout. In the dugout were Joe Girardi, manager of the Yankees, Jason Zillo, Brian Cashman, and several Yankee players—Brett Gardner, Nathan Eovaldi, and Jacoby Ellsbury to name a few. I told Joe Girardi how much respect I had for the Yankees and their organization. I said, "The Yankees are a class act." I wanted to tell him that personally.

He responded, "We're excited about what you are doing, and the awareness you're bringing is pretty amazing."

The odd thing was that I was not overwhelmed by all the Yankee players. People forget they are human beings. Many of us are just trying to make a living. No doubt they have their pitfalls and their uniqueness. But the bottom line is they are just like us. I or other people might not be able to throw or hit a ball like they do, but in our own way, we each have some very special qualities in our lives to offer.

*Hugging my son, Dante, in Yankee dugout.*

Having volunteered at many charitable organizations, I have been blessed to meet many caring and giving people. One of them was Bob, my second support driver. He is one of the kindest men and one of the most giving people I have ever met. More about this amazing individual later on. Getting back to baseball … I would rather have volunteering on my life chart than hitting a baseball five hundred feet. This is not a condemnation of professional athletes; I just feel they could be doing a lot more, yet I'm not walking in their shoes. Do you remember this from chapter 1? Of course, there are many exceptions.

I remember a story about Mariano Rivera being late coming back to lunch after taking a walk while visiting in a South American country. After time went by, his group worried and went searching for him. They located him sitting on a curb with two indigent young boys sharing his lunch. It doesn't get much better than that. I hope to travel to Cooperstown to see him enshrined.

I shook hands with Brett Gardner. I informed him that I saw him hit his first home run in spring training in Dunedin. He laughed and responded that that home run happened a long time ago.

My brother (sixty-nine years old) was shaking a pad and pencil in his hand, trying to see if he could get an autograph from some of the Yankee players. This, after telling him the day before, "Do not ask for any autographs." I told him it was not the time to seek autographs while they were practicing. I was not angry, but just kept it in perspective. Actually, it was kind of funny seeing him acting like an excited ten-year-old.

Only 750 baseball athletes in the whole world can play at the professional level. I believe they earn every penny they make.

Joe Girardi allowed me to address the whole Yankee spring training squad. They were standing on the infield grass. Joe told the team I was walking from there to Yankee Stadium. If any of them thought he was working them too hard, just think of what I was doing. Joe then presented me with a Yankees hat, shirt, and some warm-up gear. I was so grateful.

Things were really happening faster now. I did not have time to take a breath or just soak everything in. Here I was, Richard John Albero, talking to the New York Yankees team! This was a team that I had watched and admired; it was such a large part of my childhood since I was seven years old. My brother Michael (we shared a bed in a very small bedroom with my older brother Andrew) always tells the story about how I stood up in the middle of the night while sleeping and yelled out, "It's going, going, gone!" For nonbaseball folks, this was Mel Allen's (Hall of Fame Sportscaster) home run call. Baseball was in my blood!

The only thing left to start the journey was to step on home plate here at Steinbrenner Field, Tampa, Florida. I still had no clue what I was in for. My thought process was to just keep moving forward without giving tomorrow a thought. When I ended my words of inspiration to the Yankees players—at least I thought they were inspirational—I walked over to home plate, stepped on it, and uttered these words:

One small step for me,
one giant step for
all the wounded warriors' sacrifices
for our great country.
God bless them all!

*Yankee gifts.*

During my walk, depending on my physical state, weather conditions, and other factors, I tried to record an audio journal every day. *Some of these entries were lost or distorted or for various personal reasons were not transcribed. Sometimes the tapes were fragmented. I would sometimes make a brief comment, sometimes later followed by another short commentary later in the day. The tapes were not audited for grammar. The tape transcriptions are in italics and verbatim.*

## Day 1—Mileage Walked: 16.00
## (Steinbrenner Field, Tampa, Florida)

A few minutes after leaving Steinbrenner Field.

*Pretty crazy. I just left Yankee Stadium. I received a standing ovation from the New York Yankees. Joe Girardi, what a class act; the whole organization is class. A standing O. Stepped on third base. Almost coming up on my first mile. Can't believe I'm really doing this. It's going to be strange now. When I was in training, so used to turning around at the halfway point and return walking home. So it's going to be nuts. I hope Gary is watching me. I'm sure he is.* [I was crying at this point!]

A cameraman accompanied by a newspaper woman from a local TV station were following me as I started walking down Dale Mabry Road outside Steinbrenner Field. I answered their questions while walking. I was mostly saying to myself, "Man, this is pretty cool!" After a while, they departed. I was on my own! Having scouted out the Dale Mabry Road previously, I was aware of a few dangerous overpasses that had no space to walk. This would necessitate having to exit, cross another four-lane road, and come back up on top to Dale Mabry. Little did I know this was going to be a foreboding day for me, a life and death one. My almost death!

I was a little nervous at these crossings. Little did I know these crossings would be nothing compared to what was coming. At mile 6, I got my first thumbs-up for the Wounded Warrior Project from a driver. Okay! This was going to be fun. My support driver, Jimmy, came by at lunchtime with a bucket of ice to soak my feet and a hero sandwich. I was still very psyched from all the excitement of the early activities at Steinbrenner Field.

My lunchtime ritual was very important to me. I had devised a plan that was tedious, but it would keep me healthy throughout my walk. It broke down like this. After getting a heads-up call from me, my support driver would drive to my location. We would then proceed to a specific location that would have been previously scouted out by my support driver as a good place to pull over and rest. I always hoped it was somewhere nearby and in the shade. The support driver would have a bag of ice and a gallon of water in the car for me, along with my lunch order (usually a sub sandwich).

Immediately after getting picked up, I would take off my shoes, socks, sock under liners, calf compression sleeves, and knee supports. I was geared up like I was going to play a football game. Once all my gear was off, I had to take the plunge with my feet into a cold basin of water and ice. Throughout the trip, no matter how hot it was outside, I never got used to the initial plunge of my feet into that frigid water. However, if it wasn't for this icing, my feet would never have made it! After my feet soaking, lunch eaten, I would try to take a short nap. My feet were usually up on the dashboard.

Once it was time to start out for the afternoon, I would stretch and do some exercises. I had to play some real mind games with my-self. Usually I had ten to twelve miles already logged in the morning. It was a real effort for me to get out of the car knowing I had to go complete the day with another eight to ten miles of walking. I always tried to walk at least ten miles in the morning, with a goal of hopefully reaching fourteen miles. Mornings were when I felt the strongest.

Looking at the pictures included in this book, you can easily ascertain when it was an afternoon shot versus a morning shot. Pictures taken in the morning show me with my head up and good posture; afternoon shots show me with my head down and shoulders slumped. However, once on the road for the afternoon journey, after a mile or so, I usually was back into rhythm.

*In the morning.*

*In the afternoon.*

One time while soaking my feet at my lunch break, I was approached by a young lady with her puppy.

She stated, "I saw you on the internet. I only have $1.87 to give you." She then handed me the money.

I asked if she wanted some of my lunch and if the dog would like to take a drink of water from my ice bucket. She laughed and let the pup down to drink some water.

*A lady with her puppy making a donation.*

## Chapter 6

# THE RIFLE LADY (LADY, DON'T SHOOT ME!)

You cannot just go on being a good egg.
You must either hatch or go bad.
—C. S. Lewis

On the second day of the trip, a truck pulled alongside me. It held a young man accompanied by his son. He told me his son and he had seen me on the local TV news the night before. The son was so excited to meet me. They asked if they could take a picture with me. I obliged. The young boy asked for my autograph. My very first autograph! I was a star! Little did I know it would be a fleeting star.

The next morning and almost every morning after, I was up around four thirty. I had my daily ritual of saying my prayers, soaking my feet, massaging them, and making a sports drink for one of my walking bottles and lemon water for my other bottle. Then it was computer time. This was truly a nightmare for me. I had to update my website, which included putting all the new donors on my site. Next, I sent them a personal thank you via email. Finally, I checked my itinerary for local radio stations that would be calling me that day.

One of my favorite shows to be interviewed by during my walk was with Ed Randall on WFAN in New York. He was just a good human being. Ed made me feel very good after each radio chat. He was not looking just to fill a slot on his radio show. He truly had a deep appreciation of the task I was trying to accomplish. He always tried to solicit donations for my cause in a nice way. His sports radio interviews were in stark contrast to other stations, which would call me just to fill a spot. If I was ever run over and killed, they would just slip a commercial in my spot. Ed was different; he cared.

No matter how tired I was, what the weather was, or the particular road I was on, I was very meticulous every Thursday to talk at the same time with another New York radio station. Maybe I was being cynical, but toward the end of the trip, I asked this station if they could try soliciting some of their audience for donations to the Wounded Warrior Project. I informed them I did not see any donations from their audience coming in, not to mention any from themselves. The female host said she would meet me at the finish line and do a dance with me. I felt like they were just using me. No donations, no dance! I was very disappointed with them.

Every morning, I called my friend Nick (friends since the fifth grade), who eventually became my third support driver. He would send my route for the day. This was such a lifesaver. Not having to hassle with the logistics of which roads to take was a big stress relief. Anytime I needed help on my walk, Nick bailed me out, sometimes at very crucial moments. It was always a great feeling when I called Nick to scout out a shortcut or a route off the main roads, and he came up with one.

My breakfast was usually at Cracker Barrel or at the hotel where I stayed. When at the hotel's breakfast buffet, I became an expert at making waffles on the grill! My order was always pretty much the same: two eggs sunny-side up, ham, hash browns, two pancakes, waffle, grits or farina, white toast. People always ask me when they hear about my walk how much weight I lost. Pretty amazingly, I started my walk weighing 187 pounds and ended my walk weighing 187 pounds. With this being said, looking at pictures of doing my walk, my weight was well distributed, not like today, where unfortunately it shows in my belly!

*A typical morning breakfast!*

*A typical evening dinner!*

The second most-asked question after I completed my walk was how many sneakers I wore through. I started with nine pairs of shoes. I named them after Yankee players. Of course, my first pair of shoes was called Babe Ruth. I rotated the shoes every morning and afternoon, starting with a different pair the next day. Eventually, I wore out four complete pairs; the other five pairs were partially worn out. The first pair eventually got bronzed. This set of shoes is now hanging on my office wall. The second pair of shoes was also bronzed. This pair was presented as a gift to Andrew Levy in gratitude for his support during my walk.

*My walking shoes.*

The next issue was returning to my pickup point. Be it after lunchtime or the next morning, returning to the exact spot where I had been picked up needed a system in itself. It sounds easy, but when you are in the middle of nowhere, such as in a forest, it's difficult to find your previous spot. Sometimes I would hang a bright kerchief on a tree branch that we could spot from the road when returning.

Day two had nothing noteworthy except for a few odds and ends. Jimmy went to drop me off at the spot he had picked me up the previous afternoon. However, he couldn't pull in. Jimmy said he would drop me off a hundred yards down the road. I told him I would walk back to the exact spot where he had picked me up the previous afternoon. I did not want anybody with a phone camera or whatever tracking me and seeing me start at a different spot. I was real anal about this. I didn't want to be accused of cheating. So I walked back to the exact starting point from the day before and began day 2.

My walking app informed me I had logged sixteen miles. Notice I did not mention the app by name. This company did not donate to my walk. It still bothers me that this company and other companies would not sponsor me. I thought my walk was for such a good cause. From my point of view, they could give me support without any financial loss. Most likely, they would financially gain from the exposure of supporting my walk. I just could not come to terms with this lack of support.

I started day three of my walk and every day afterward with a raise of my arm straight up and then a fist bump up to the sky. Not every morning, but on certain mornings when I had a certain cloud formation, I would visualize my mother, my grandmother, and Gary sitting on a cloud watching me. This became a regular morning ritual until I hit Ocala. Then I adjusted this routine.

You might ask how my grandmother gets into the picture. Hopefully this little story will explain why. I was at a teaching conference a few years before my retirement. The facilitator started with this icebreaker: If you had to be anywhere at this moment, a certain place, where would you choose? She started asking various teachers one after another. To name a few, some of the responses were the French Riviera, Italy, Swiss Alps, and Paris. My turn came. My response was my grandmother's lap. I told the participants my grandmother's lap was the safest place in the world. When I sat in her lap, everything was right and safe in the world! My grandmother could not read, write, or speak English. What she lacked in formal education, she made up a million times over with her love for her daughter, Lucy, and her grandchildren. As a little side note, she loved the music from a hit song "Open the Door, Richard." Hence, the origins of my name.

## Day 2—Mileage Walked: 16.00 (Land O' Lakes, Florida)

*I'm on Route 41. I have sixteen miles logged in. Will be on Route 41 for most of the day today. God be with me.*

## Day 3—MIleage Walked: 15.05 (Shady Hills, Florida)

*Just got dropped off; it's about eight thirty. Just started my walk, high fisted the sky. I have to be nuts for doing this! It's going to be around eighty something today. The fog is clearing, which is a good sign.*

*Afternoon: Well, having a drink of my sports water. It looks like it's going to need a little vodka as this walk gets longer.*

## Day 4—Mileage Walked: 15.09
## (South Brooksville, Florida)

My day started at Turner Funeral Home. I was hoping this was not going to be a bad omen. Not that I was superstitious or anything. However, when I was coaching football at the secondary level, there was one team I could never beat. No matter how good my team was or how bad they were, I would always lose to them. My assistant coach had a theory. We lost every year because our team bus passed a cemetery located a short distance from the football field. This was our source of bad luck. The next time we played them, I had the bus driver stop in front of the cemetery. We opened the gates and proceeded to the field. Guess what? We won that game! Who can figure it?

## Day 5—Mileage Walked: 9.67 (Floral City, Florida)

*Stopping at this farm with a whole bunch of bulls, some really big-ass bulls, all looking at me. Hey guys, how are you doing? You look like the big three: Mantle, Gehrig, and Ruth. All right, I have walking to do, boys. Hate to tell you, but you're going to make some nice hamburgers someday.*

*Afternoon: Hate to say it, Richard—you stink!*

On this particular day, I was walking past a little pond on the right side of a desolate driveway. The pond had beautiful flowers and woods surrounding it. The pond was so picturesque. I took a couple of pictures with my camera. Then I continued walking on the side of the road, which had muddy grass. Suddenly, after a few minutes at the most, I heard a speeding vehicle.

I turned and saw it was an old truck. The driver was a woman.

She passed me, saw me and hit the brakes, and then U-turned it. Now she was on the grassy knoll that I was walking on, with the truck facing me.

She stopped the truck, jumped out with a shotgun in her hand, and aimed it at me. She yelled, "What are you doing taking pictures of my property?"

I looked at her and said, "It's pretty."

She was dumbfounded (actually I think she was dumb before this!) and raised the rifle a little higher.

I responded and said, "Hold on!" I then very quickly told her about my walk for the Wounded Warrior Project. When I was done, she still had a confused look on her face. I very cautiously handed her one of my Wounded Warrior cards that I had printed.

She looked at the card and threw it onto the seat of her truck. She said, "No more pictures," and hopped into the truck.

I yelled back, "Okay, no more pictures." The best I could figure out was maybe she had a meth lab back in the woods and probably thought I was casing the place. Thank God she didn't shoot my butt!

**Late Morning, Day 5**

*Yee Yang Yo Yang, what is that on the side of the road? Hope it's not a body.*

I estimate on my walk I probably passed at least fifty or more memorial markers on the side of the roads. These markers were placed in remembrance of somebody who died at that particular spot. At each marker, my ritual was to stop and say three Hail Marys, along with a small prayer for their family's well-being. Having said these prayers, my hope for these families was that they feel less pain for their loss of a loved one. Another ritual I had was never to step on a grid gate in the road. I always had the fear the grate would sink under my weight. I would fall below, never to be seen again!

**Midday, Day 5**

*Ah! Breeze blowing, beautiful forest on each side. Reminds me of when I was a little kid romping in the woods. Can't get any better than this except for the blisters on my toes, not too much traffic, and one foot ahead of the other. Ocala, here I come.*

Little did I know that I would be moving to Ocala after my walk was complete.

## Late Afternoon, Day 5

*Urinating in the woods, I just noticed a barbed wire fence next to me. Hopefully not electrified; I would light up like a Christmas tree. I think it's to keep the Communists out!*

*What a beautiful country. God bless America is all I can say. That's all I can say!*

*I can't believe I'm finally making it to the top of this hill. If there are more hills after this, I think I'm going to scream Yow!*

Little did I know this would be a foreboding of what was waiting for me in Virginia—forty-nine hills to walk up in two days.

At lunchtime, I came upon a VFW building. I was so excited. I thought no doubt I would get a real big welcome and hopefully receive some donations. Boy, was I wrong! I cannot describe how disappointed I was. I walked in. The person in charge, a lady, approached me. I told her about my walk and asked if I could address the patrons. Most of them were drinking and smoking at the bar. I also asked if my support driver could come in for a drink of water. She told me he could not, because he was not a member, but that I could stay as an ex–naval officer. Nor could I address the patrons soliciting any kind of donations. She told me I could come back later that night and talk to the man in charge of the VFW. I responded this was not possible, as I had several more miles to walk that day. She was so disingenuous. I was so disappointed after being on a high from all the kind people I had met so far on my walk.

# Day 6—Mileage Walked: 15.11 (Inverness, Florida)

*Early morning: Lord, keep me safe today. Get Saint Christopher out of bed and have him watch over me as well. All right, here we go!*

*Morning: Starting at East New Jersey Trail in Floral City. It's raining; starting my first test of the metal. Wish me luck. Goodbye.*

*Afternoon: The rain is stopping. Thank God I have a sweatshirt on.*

*I'm in redneck alley. It's unbelievable. Don't know why my little toe is starting to hurt again, but it is what it is. I'm sucking it up, putting one foot ahead of the other.*

*I never thought I'd get this excited about changing roads. I just hit Route 44 in Inverness. I'm now taking a right turn on Route 44. The first sign I see is a sign for Wildwood, nineteen miles. I'm now heading east.*

*I'm on Trample Court in Inverness. I will be walking on Gulf to Lake Highway, which is Route 44, heading to Route 301. Wish me luck. God keep me safe.*

*Gary, hope you're up there watching me* [crying]. *Man, I know I have a ways to go. I'll be up there in New York for your memorial. Keep me safe. I love you.*

The following recording is an interview of me by me. Just one week out and already getting punchy!

*Afternoon: All right, Richard Albero. Welcome to Citrus County, walking for the Wounded Warrior Project in honor of Gary Albero. Can you tell us why you are doing this?*

*Yeah, because I am nuts. Sometimes I should think of things before I get myself into things like this. That's all right. Sky is blue, sun is coming out, and my feet don't hurt at least for a little while; no cars are trying to run me over. Can't get much better than this. All right, let's go, feet. Crow making noise in the background. Yawk, yawk, yawk* [me yelling these words].

*Taking off the bottle cap to my Sports Water.* (Note: Sports Water was a company located in Connecticut that donated a constant supply of bottled water throughout my trip. I was extremely thankful for this support.) *I was going to throw it in the woods, but I don't pollute. I love my country.*

*Don't get too fat, boys. They will make hamburgers out of you. Glad you're eating the good stuff, keeping that grass fed.* (While looking at some bulls on some farmland.)

## Day 7—Rest Day, Mileage Walked: 0

Today is Sunday. It was a rest day. Eventually I would get smarter and realize there was less traffic on Sunday. I would adjust my day off to Wednesday and then walk on Sunday.

## Interlude 1

> Friendship isn't a big thing—
> It's a million little things.

I was very fortunate to have some very special people be my support drivers throughout my walk. I had such trust and faith with them being at my side during my walk. These support drivers were such a comfort factor. In the morning, I would always kneel down to say my prayers. I would ask God to keep me alive for that day's walk. Once in a while, one of my support drivers would walk out of the bathroom and observe me praying. By their expressions, I think it shocked them I was that comfortable praying in front of them. In a good way, I believe it may have reaffirmed their faith.

## Jimmy

Jimmy was my first support driver. I had known Jimmy since he was four years old. We competed many times against each other into our teen years. We attended the same parochial grammar and high school. Jimmy was born on April 1. Whether that had any bearing on him breaking thirty bones in his body, I don't know. I have to admit to breaking one of those bones when Jimmy fell off his bike. Unfortunately, I ran over his arm. Maybe all those trips to the hospital was why he eventually became COO of a major hospital in New Jersey.

In his heart, Jimmy in a lot of ways wanted to be like me. In a lot of ways he did not want to be like me! Regardless, after I completed my walk, Jimmy had a new sense of respect for me. We both had the same sense of faith and, I believe, love for our country.

Here's a short story about Jimmy. The X-ray technicians at his hospital were out sick one day. So Jimmy went down to help some of the wheelchair patients. One of the patients, an older, frail woman, asked Jimmy what he did at the hospital. She couldn't believe he was the COO and helping push wheelchairs. Jimmy eventually helped her set up an annuity to help her with her finances. In addition, he continued to visit her regularly until her death. By the way, she donated $250,000 to the hospital in Jimmy's name.

Here's an excerpt from an interview with Jimmy during my walk.

*Rich attracted a lot of crazy drivers, a lot of trucks, and weird people who came out with a gun or something one of these days. You never know how it will be when he gets into rougher country up in Georgia and some of the other states. We'll see; hopefully he will make it without any problems.*

## Day 8, Week 2—Mileage Walked: 16.86 (Wildwood, Florida)

*Okay, week 2 of my voyage. Still feeling strong. Have a nice early start; Bob Warner is my support driver. Hope Jimmy is okay staying at my house with Dante. He is probably getting real excited for the Yankee Party. Staying in the same place, which is really nice. I'm walking on Route 475 heading toward Hawthorn, Florida. Heading out of Ocala, I'm passing all kinds of horse farms, cattle farms, and even some with goats. They all come out and greet me with their bells on. Absolutely pretty. Seen some roadkills as well, unfortunately. All right, God keep me safe.*

## Day 9—Mileage Walked: 15.48 (Ocala, Florida)

*About a mile into my walk on Route 475 north heading to Hawthorne. Passed the one-hundred-mile marker yesterday. So things are going pretty well. Some minor pains here and there. But that's what life is all about. All right, power to the people.*

*Feeling a little low but just saw a sign that said Jacksonville 62 miles, which gave me a boost in my step. I'm on Route 20 in the country more or less, and have safety on the side of the road and off this horrendous Route 301. Bob, my support driver, has been great. Sun rising; it's a great day. Hopefully God's watching over me. Wish me the best.*

*[Yelling with joy.] Sidewalks, sidewalks, I never thought I'd be so happy to see a sidewalk. Hey, all right!*

### That Evening Checking into My Hotel Room

*I'm at the front desk of my hotel, telling a person about my walk from Tampa to the Bronx. These two guys are listening standing next to us.*

One guy said, *"You're walking from Tampa to the Bronx?"* He looks at the other guy, who asks. *"Where is the Bronx?"* His friend says, *"You idiot. The Bronx is in Brooklyn. Everybody knows that!"*

You can't make this stuff up!

*Chapter 7*

# THE YANKEE PARTY

Gratitude is a sign of noble souls.
—Aesop

Every year at the end of spring training, Andrew Levy would sponsor a Yankee party on a lagoon in Clearwater, Florida. This party was by invitation only, which included several past Yankee greats, the Yankee manager, and other celebrities. I was invited as one of the star attendees. I was extremely excited to attend the Yankee party that Wednesday night, March 11. I was going to meet several retired Yankees I adored watching when I was younger.

*Andrew Levy and I at the Yankee Party.*

I did get my walk of 10.57 miles in that morning. Bob was driving me back to my house in Dunedin from Citra. My plan was to sleep at my house in Dunedin in order to save on a hotel bill and see Molly, my loving Saint Bernard, plus check on Dante, my son. Hopefully, he still had my house and car in one piece! The next morning I would drive back to Citra and begin walking that afternoon, on the twelfth. So in essence, I would only lose one day off my schedule, which I could make up by skipping one of my off days. At least that was the plan!

I thought and believed this would be my last day with Jimmy as my support driver. Little did I know he would bail me out later in my walk. He would be my last support driver as I completed the final few days of my adventure in New Jersey.

When we drove up my driveway in Dunedin Wednesday afternoon, I began unloading bags from the car. My next-door neighbor saw me. His first words were not "Hi," but "Did you quit already?" Those words hit me like a ton of bricks. I was really disappointed in him, but at the same time, it just made me even more determined to complete the walk. So many people—friends, relatives, reporters, and so on—did not know me as well as they thought. They did not know my soul, my faith in God, my faith in Gary, my faith in what's good in this world. I owed it to the wounded warriors to complete this trip for all the pain and hardships they endured to make our country great. My neighbor's comment was the shot in the ass I needed to be even more convinced I would complete this adventure.

When I arrived at the party, I met Andrew for the first time in person. We smiled at each other and hugged. I was really excited. We loaded thirty cases of Sports Water into Bob's car. Bob would become my second support driver for the following week. I had met Bob as a volunteer at Saint Vincent de Paul food pantry in Dunedin, Florida.

The party was unbelievable. In attendance were all these Yankee greats that I had admired since I was a kid. I met Ron Guidry, one of the greatest Yankee pitchers. I told him about my walk. He looked me straight in the eyes and said what a great thing I was doing. Also, how important my walk was. He said, "I'm very proud of you and what you're doing." Next, I met Mickey Rivers, whom I would eventually meet again when my walk was over at Yankee Stadium.

Andrew walked me over to greet Joe Girardi and take some

pictures with him. Joe asked how I was doing. I said it was getting tough. "Hope I make it through."

Joe responded, "Don't worry; I will see you in the Bronx!" After my neighbor's comment, this made me feel so good! Hell, if the manager of the Yankees thought I could do it, what else did I need? Am I a Yankees fan or what? I introduced Joe to my son, Dante. He told Dante his son had the same name. He made Dante feel so comfortable. Joe spoke to him for about fifteen minutes. During this time, Joe was getting hassled by fans at the party wanting to take a picture with him. I enjoyed being with Joe not because he was the Yankee manager, but because I knew he was not only a good person, but a good family man as well.

In regard to pictures, all these people were coming up to me after I was introduced at the podium by the master of ceremonies. He told the crowd about my walk. I had no complaints. Several women, politicians, and firefighters approached me immediately afterward, asking if they could take a picture together with me. My only regret was not taking pictures on my phone. It was such a whirlwind, my head was spinning, and my body was tired and still adjusting to the routine of the walk. Also, it was getting late for me. I had to watch what I was drinking. They had an open bar with several different types of top-shelf liquor. It was very rewarding watching Jimmy and Bob relishing the party festivities. They were so starstruck. In a way, it was funny watching their facial expressions throughout the night.

I wished things would slow down so I could just take things in. The party events were moving so fast and getting faster. People every minute were coming up to me. "Can we take a picture?" I mean, who was I? I never really thought about the actual walk as something bad-ass but just a chance to do some good. It seemed pretty simple to me. Why were all these people going nuts about it?

Finally, it was time to leave. I gave Andrew a hug. He asked if I needed anything. My response was a very personal one. Andrew and I would soon become closer friends as my adventure unfolded. Andrew would get to know me as a good person, and I would get to know Andrew as a good person as well.

## Day 10—No Audio, Mileage Walked: 10.57 (Citra, Florida)

*Chapter 8*

# ONE FOOT AHEAD OF THE OTHER

There is no security on earth;
There is only opportunity!
—General Douglas MacArthur

## Day 11—Mileage Walked: 10.02 (Citra, Florida)

*Well, let's see. Today is Thursday, March 12. Route 301 heading toward Hawthorne about eight miles out, and then it's a right turn to Jacksonville. Not too much traffic. Still a few nuts on the road. Had the Yankee party last night: Joe Girardi, Goose Gossage, Mickey Rivers, Lee Mazzilli, Jason Zillo, Ron Guidry, sure there were others. Okay, I have to get off and tie my shoelaces.*

Looking back over this entry, I was surprised it was so short. I asked myself why I didn't expound more on the party with all the celebrities in attendance. But in retrospect, I was out of my routine, up late with the party, had a new support driver, and my body was dragging.

## Day 12—No Audio, Mileage Walked: 17.04 (Melrose, Florida)

## Day 13—Mileage Walked: 16.13 (Keystone Heights, Florida)

*You always think when you first start out, you can do fifteen miles today. It's early in the morning, but then when you get up around seven, reality sets in. I'm in Keystone, Florida, on Route 21 just about forty-five miles south of Jacksonville. Tomorrow is a day off; I can't wait. I'll have two weeks logged on the road; ten more to go.*

## Day 14—Rest Day, Mileage Walked: 0

Several moments while Bob was my support driver are worth mentioning. The first event was when we were staying at a motel displaying a big sign in front of it saying, "We support our troops!" I went up to the manager and informed him about my walk. I also informed him I had been a naval officer. I was sure that I would get a discounted rate, maybe even the room for free. Boy, was I mistaken. He said, "No, that is the rate!" I just turned around, took another look at the sign, and walked away, shaking my head!

The second incident, which was one of the most endearing events of the trip, was that we had a room booked in Gainesville for a very good, low rate. Unfortunately, we were a day behind and had to re-book the room for the next day. Well, little did I know that a big race car event was going on in Gainesville for that particular night. The manager informed us he had a room available; however, the new rate was three times the cost of the original rate. Money for me was very tight. I was financing the total trip at this point on my own. Every penny I could save on hotel bills would be critical. (Eventually the Wounded Warrior Project would come to my rescue.) I could not get him to budge on the rate. Being exhausted, I just faced reality and had to pay the rip-off price. Also, the room was on the second floor, with no elevators. I had to lug all my stuff up a flight of stairs. My stuff included my mixer and all my walking shoes, my iPad, first aid equipment, boxes of Epsom salts, exercise bands, and many other little incidentals.

I still have a very vivid memory of Bob and me lugging all our stuff up those stairs. After walking almost twenty miles that day, it was pretty exhausting. While I was at the desk booking the room and trying to get the manager to give me a break on the price, I noticed a door behind the front desk was open to a laundry room. One of the maids in her uniform was listening to me begging the manager for a better rate. As I started to leave, she came up to me and handed me a check for fifty dollars for the Wounded Warrior Project. She said she had two sons in the navy serving overseas. She stated she didn't have much money but hoped this would help. I had tears in my eyes and just hugged her and said thank you. I then walked past the schmuck behind the desk and went to unload Bob's car.

**Interlude 2**

A true friend is one who overlooks your
failures and tolerates your success!
—Doug Larson

**Bob**

I met Bob volunteering at a Saint Vincent de Paul food pantry in Dunedin, Florida. I never in my life met a more caring or giving person. The food pantry had a rule that none of our personal money could be given to the clients. However, I cannot tell you how many times Bob took money out of his own pocket to support these clients who were down on their luck. I remember one young lady who said her tires were so bad that she could hardly ride on them. She had a young baby in her arms. Bob immediately reached into his pocket and gave her enough money to buy the tires. I would tell him that some of the clients were just taking advantage of him. He would just smile and respond, "I know, but if they need help, I will help them."

At Christmastime, Bob and I would buy some blankets and gift cards from McDonalds. We would drive into Clearwater and drive around giving the gift cards and blankets out to the homeless. Another year we gave out gloves and shirts. Bob was always willing to join me on these adventures.

As I said before and it is worth repeating, I never met a more giving and kinder person in my life. God bless him!

Here are a couple of excerpts from my interview with Bob before he returned home.

*I ask the Good Lord to take care of you when walking down those roads the way those cars come by. He needs to be with you the whole trip.*

*My biggest surprise was how long fifteen miles is! I applaud you for you to go that many miles. It's a long way. I get in my car, and every mile seems like ten miles. So I applaud you for what you're doing. I was surprised first of all by all the equipment you needed to take with you to do this walk. It's a big responsibility for me, and I take it very seriously. I gotta tell you it's been an honor to do what I did. Thanks again.*

**At the end of the day, taking my gear to the hotel room.**

*Chapter 9*

# MIKEY AND JACKSONVILLE

Any day I wake up is a good day.
—Duke Ellington

## Day 15, Week 3—Mileage Walked: 16.97
## (Asbury Lake and Middlebury, Florida)

*I'm dragging ass, and there is a big bad boy hill in front of me, a bunch
of trucks coming down. It's going to be a bitch. Well, there are a lot of
bitches. I guess it's not nice to say, cancel, cancel. I'm going to try to do
this.*

*A Monday, about fifteen miles out of Jacksonville, in Orange Park,
Florida. My brother Michael is now my new support driver. He seems to
be doing pretty well for the first day. I'm doing pretty well myself. Seem
to be pretty strong, still some nuts on the road. Okay, God be with me.*

*Dragging ass* was a term I used many times during my walk. A reporter asked me what I meant by that term. My response was, "Think
about when your mind is so stressed out from constant concentration
trying to stay alive, everything around you becomes boring, and your
body just doesn't want to take another step."

What people did not realize about my walk was the skill set
necessary to be successful. Every car that approached me, I had
to put a visual fix on. I lost count of how many people veered off
the road, almost hitting me. The drivers were either talking on the
phone, texting, putting makeup on, reading the paper (yes, reading
the paper!), putting drops into their eyes, or something else. These

54

were only some of the drivers' crazy actions. I must reiterate this fact. Sometimes I only had a foot on the side of the road to navigate. Usually next to me was a steep incline down into a stream or a ditch.

One particular incident I can still recall very vividly. A large pickup truck had several pieces of furniture loaded in the back bed stacked very high above the front cab.

Notice I didn't say secured in the back bed. As it passed me and made a slight turn to its left, I heard a rumble of noise. I looked toward the road behind me for the source of the noise. Immediately, two chairs were rolling at me, and a table was flying in the air at me! I literally had to jump into the ditch next to me to avoid a nasty collision with the furniture.

Another time, I was actually blown off my feet backward. Not to mention when I was blown sideways down an embankment into a muddy ditch by the force of a huge truck speeding past me doing at least seventy-five miles per hour. The worst roadway was Route 17 coming out of Savannah. I recall calling my friend Nick and begging him to locate an alternative route for me. I had to get off this death trap.

## Day 16—Mileage Walked: 13.84 (Lakeside and Bellair-Meadowbrook Terrace, Florida)

*Leaving Orangeburg, Florida. Heading toward Jacksonville. Hitting the two-hundred-mile mark. Today is Saint Patty's Day. I thought of painting my sneakers green, but that would wreck them. I have a radio interview, which is cool. I have sidewalks most of the way, which makes it nice. It's getting hot. So hopefully I will be in Georgia soon.*

My first day walking in Jacksonville was an adventure. While I was walking, a man in his early twenties, dressed in a white shirt and tie, came running out toward me from a nearby small store. He asked what I was doing as he strolled beside me. I told him that I was walking to New York. He then repeated his question and asked what I was really doing. I went into a little more detail, still trying to convince him I was walking from Tampa to the Bronx. He asked if I was in the service. I said, "Yes. I retired as a lieutenant (junior grade) from the United States Navy.

He then said, "Well, you're going to get your ass capped walking around this area."

I said. "Seriously?"

He then proceeded to slide back his shirtsleeve, revealing a huge knife fastened to his arm with the point in his open palm facing me. He then stated, "I'm not kidding; your ass is going to get capped."

At that moment I was so focused on my walking, I failed to observe my surroundings. Every other shop seemed to be some kind of car repair shop next to a dilapidated building. He then informed me he had to get back to work. He wished me luck. Well, I immediately started imitating an owl, constantly rotating my head from side to side taking everything into view. I was nervous but not scared, ready to act if I had to. Many of my associates had recommended that I should be carrying a gun with me. I totally rejected this idea for several different reasons.

I came to a T in the road and made a right turn. The area seemed a little better, but then I realized my water bottle was empty. Worse, my phone was almost dead. I couldn't contact my brother Mikey! So I just kept walking, hoping my brother would come along. He did have my route, right?

After about another twenty minutes of walking, I started to get worried. No water, and my body temperature was escalating. Then I saw a railroad boxcar with all kinds of motorcycle decal stuff displayed on it. Nervous, but without much choice, I knocked on the door of the boxcar and entered. Well, three very tough-looking motorcycle guys with long hair and a lot of tattoos were standing at a counter eating pizza. I just said, "Hey, guys," and walked in. I explained to them about my walk. They were pretty impressed. They shared with me some of their water and pizza. They let me charge my phone. Phone charged, I finally was able to make contact with my brother. The motorcycle guys gave me directions to the shop for my brother to follow. Thankfully, Mikey found the shop. As we continued to chat, they told me the road I was traveling on would end. They knew of a good shortcut through a nice neighborhood leading into the center of Jacksonville. I wanted to kiss them! God knows if I had, what part of Jacksonville my body parts would be in! I told them that I was going to give them a shout-out about their business on Facebook and Twitter, which I did the next morning before my walk. The shortcut they showed me allowed me to relax a little, get off the main road, and avoid the dangerous areas of Jacksonville.

March 18, 2015, is a day that I will always remember. I had an appointment to visit the main office of the Wounded Warrior Project in Jacksonville, Florida. My brother and I drove from the motel and parked the car. As we approached the office, two men were walking outside in the office park. Seeing us, they approached.

One gentleman introduced himself as Steven Nardizzi, CEO of the Wounded Warrior Project. He asked, "Are you Richard?"

I said, "I am."

We chatted for a while. Mr. Nardizzi told me how proud the Wounded Warrior Project was of me. We then proceeded to enter the building. Two large doors, floor to ceiling in height, were closed and blocking our entrance. Mr. Nardizzi opened the large doors. I stepped inside into a huge two-floor room. It was a large foyer space with an upper balcony. I proceeded into this room, where every employee of the Wounded Warrior Project office of Jacksonville was in attendance. Employees were on the stairs, in the hallway, on the upper floor, and standing in front of me. Mr. Nardizzi introduced me. Mikey was very gracious, put an arm around my back, and pushed me forward. I was never so overwhelmed. The only comparable feeling I could think of was entering a boxing ring in college and getting hit by all the bright lights. Unfortunately, I got hit by my boxing opponent that night as well!

I just remember saying thank you, with tears coming from my eyes and rolling down my cheeks. It was so heartwarming. I could not figure out why they were clapping for me. In my mind, I was just a guy walking to the Bronx trying to do some good for the wounded warriors and paying homage to my nephew Gary. At this moment, the realization hit me: this was no small feat that I was trying to accomplish.

Afterward, I was introduced to Al Giordano, COO of the Wounded Warrior Project. We went into an office and chatted. He asked me how the Wounded Warrior Project could assist me. I just chuckled. Mikey gave me a look. I was very straightforward with him. "To start off with, could I have a shirt with the Wounded Warrior logo on it, and maybe some kind of rain jacket? Oh, and maybe a hat." I told him the hotel room costs were killing me. In order to save costs, I was staying in some very dumpy places. Also, the food costs were hitting my pocketbook pretty hard.

Mr. Giordano chatted with me about logistics. My prayers were answered. He said they would assist me with my difficulties. Also, Mr. Giordano told me about his son, who was going to attend the United States Merchant Marine Academy. I am an alum of the USMMA. Mr. Giordano had some contacts with the academy. He said he would get some assistance and PR for me along my route from them. Unfortunately, this never came to fruition. The academy did put a little blurb about me in their alum magazine, though.

After a half hour, a person came in carrying a duffel bag. Inside were several shirts, a raincoat, and two hats, all with the Wounded Warrior logo. I was like a pig in heaven. It even got better. Mr. Giordano said they would help me out with some of my expenses by trying to get a donor to cover my hotel costs.

Shortly after, I was introduced to Dan, who gave me a tour of the facility. I was so impressed by the information exhibited in the Wounded Warrior Project building and what they were doing to assist our military personnel. As we proceeded walking through the various offices, many employees stood up and shook my hand. Finally, we stopped in front of a big logo on the wall of the Wounded Warrior Project. Dan said, "You see that guy on the bottom carrying the soldier?"

I said, "Yes."

He said, "Well, that's you." I couldn't believe he was equating me to a soldier doing such a heroic act. I just looked at him in disbelief. Dan said what I was doing with this walk was heroic. I was and still am overwhelmed by his statement.

Finally, before leaving, I was introduced to a group of wounded warriors. I sat down and had a conversation with them. One thing that stood out to me was a comment by one particular warrior. He remembered when he was in Iraq. Congress was running out of funds to support our armed forces. The government could not finance protective equipment in both the Iraq and Afghanistan theaters. Consequently, the soldiers were ordered to turn in their protective equipment. This gear would be shipped to fellow soldiers in Afghanistan. To replace the gear they were forced to give up, they improvised by filling small sandbags and hanging them around their backs and chests for protection! I was totally flabbergasted.

*Wounded Warrior Project Office, Jacksonville, Florida.*

As we were ending our tour, ascending a flight of stairs, I noticed Dan was slowing down a little bit. I asked him if he was okay. He responded that he had to go a little slow up stairs and pulled up his pant legs. He was a double amputee. I was shocked! Up to that moment, I would never have guessed Dan was a double amputee. My heart went out to him. I was thinking my walk was nothing compared to what these guys went through. Later during my walk, when I felt tired, depressed, and just beat up, I thought of that moment when Dan showed me his legs. It was not only the loss of his legs, but the knowledge of how much he loved our country. I said to myself many times during my walk in moments of despair, "Think of the wounded warriors and stop bitching!"

## Day 17—Mileage Walked: 0 (Jacksonville, Florida)

*Well, today I went to the main Wounded Warrior Project in Jacksonville, Florida. I cannot put in words the feelings I have. I met Dan, who lost both legs fighting for our country. He was just a wonderful individual. He invited me to go down and visit those wounded warriors rehabilitating in a DC hospital, thinking I could be helpful. I told him I would try to do it. He said he would teach me yoga in return. I met Mr. Nardizzi and Al Giordano. All the people were so wonderful to me. When I walked into the building, they had every employee at the entrance, down the hallways, and up the stairs, giving me a standing ovation.*

*I still cannot comprehend all the feelings that I have. Still processing as I learn more about myself. I just want to be able to keep walking and hope that real good comes out of this. People who are hurting will maybe be in a better place. I pray to God to keep me safe. I was just amazed how everybody in the place had such a nice attitude, smiling, coming over to me. Yet I didn't feel like I was doing anything great. I'm just trying to show what a great country we have here.*

*Later that night …*

*So, hmm, wanted to get this down. It's one o'clock. I'm normally in bed at eight o'clock at the latest, but I'm just so pumped up, I can't sleep. It's time we find the goodness in people is more prominent than, let's say, the badness in people. My thoughts are with all the wounded warriors. There is somebody out there caring for them. I'm really starting to feel like I'm a crusader. Maybe I'm a crusader for them. My prayers go out for all of them. I'd better get to bed.*

## Day 18—Mileage Walked: 10.05 (Jacksonville, Florida)

*Okay, after a year of planning, looking at Jacksonville, this means my first main stop. Now hitting Main Street, taking a left turn, which is Route 17. I'm staying on that baby all the way to Savannah. Hopefully, all the people who thought I was ready to go out to pasture have second thoughts now. My soul feels good!*

During my time in Jacksonville, I received a phone call from Andrew Levy. He told me that a major TV network morning show wanted to air a piece on me. I was so excited. Hell, who doesn't want to be a TV star? Little did I know that the next week was going to be a *Rocky Horror Picture Show.*

The next day at my hotel room, I was introduced to the producer, a cameraman, and a soundman from the morning show. The producer, whom I will only refer to as a very overzealous individual (being extremely kind here!), said they would follow me around and do some interviewing. I thought to myself, a piece of cake. Little did I know that within a few days I would be ready to strangle this producer—that is, if my brother Mikey didn't do it first. It didn't take him long to take a strong dislike to this producer. Now in her defense, she was probably doing her job to get the piece done quickly.

Since I was coming up to the three-week marker of my walk, I already had a set routine. I knew it had to be that way for me to succeed in this adventure. I will only mention a few of the many disagreements I had with this producer.

The first was she wanted to film me at my lunch break. No problem! Okay, easy, follow me, and when I stop for lunch, ask me a few questions on my break. So, while on my walk, after doing about thirteen miles during a hot morning, I found a little grassy hill on the side of a fish store parking lot. Mikey came by with my food and a bucket of ice with water to soak my feet. Soon after, I got a call from the morning show producer. I informed her I was getting ready to eat my lunch and prepare for the afternoon segment of my walk.

She said, "Don't eat yet; we are waiting to eat at a restaurant here. We will come to you in about forty-five minutes to film after we finish eating our lunch."

I said, "Are you kidding me? I can't wait that long. I have to get on the road." Well, they showed up in about thirty-five minutes.

They applied makeup on me and did their interview with me sitting on a chair under a tree. Then I had to change into different clothing so it looked like a different day. They filmed me walking down a road by the fish store. This interview delayed me from getting out for the afternoon jaunt by at least an hour and a half. I knew my body would pay the price for this. It did!

Incident number two: I got a call that same evening from the producer saying they were at their hotel. She would come over around nine for another interview.

I said, "Lady, it's almost seven thirty. I'm already late getting to bed because of you from my afternoon walk. Now you want me to delay my bedtime for ninety minutes? No way!" and ended the conversation. I knew she was trying to do her job, but I also knew that I needed to stay on a strict routine to be successful. At this point, if they promised me a movie contract with her being the producer, I would have said no, along with a few other choice words.

Three side notes on my time with the morning show film crew. First, the cameraman was kind of distant from me in the beginning. He was very attentive to his job. However, the last day before the filming was over, he pulled me aside. After filming me these last few days, he shared with me how much respect he had for me now. He realized how hard it was for me doing this walk after firsthand watching my preparation, fighting the traffic and rough roads. He gave me a donation for the Wounded Warrior Project.

The producer kept emailing me with updates about when my interview would air on TV. I appreciated this. Who didn't want to see themselves on TV? So that morning, I delayed the start to my walk, again knocking me out of my all-important routine. I watched the entire morning show to see my clip. It didn't happen. This scenario repeated itself for each of the next three days. In all honesty, I was looking for an ego boost by seeing myself on TV.

These late starts in the morning were throwing off my morning routine and driving me crazy. Finally, on the following Saturday morning, less than a one-minute clip of my walk aired. I was shocked by my appearance. I could not believe all the aggravation, time, and effort that went into this clip. I looked like hell. Heck, I thought *60 Minutes* should have been doing a segment on me. After dealing with this producer, I didn't think I would have accepted an invitation from *60 Minutes* even if they offered! I know what you're thinking. Yes, I would. In truth, yes, but truly not with this overzealous producer!

Also, as I was reviewing my journal tapes, I realized I did not make one entry about the TV morning show crew. On reflection, the producer had thrown my schedule so out of whack that when I did get back to the hotel room, I just wanted to go to bed. As a disclaimer, the producer was just doing her job.

## Day 19—Mileage Walked: 17.81 (Jacksonville and Yulee, Florida)

*I'm finally getting out of Jacksonville and heading up to Yulee. I'm starting my walk over an overpass, which is not the best way to start. I think I'm done with all the hoopla now. I can start walking. My body is a little down. I actually slept till six o'clock. Caught a cold. Have to start eating better and get my body in better shape. All right, wish me a safe day.*

One last note on my last day in Jacksonville ... Walking out, I wasn't sure I was on the right road. So I stopped at a fast-food place. I went up to two girls who were working at the establishment. I asked them if this was the right road. I told them I was walking to New York.

After they confirmed I was on the right road, one of the girls told me that even though I was on the correct road, I would not get to New York that night.

I said, "That's okay; I'll probably make it to New York tomorrow." She responded, "That's good."

I smiled and left. You can't make this stuff up.

## Day 20—Mileage Walked: 10.61 (Yulee, Florida)

*I could possibly hit Georgia today, which would be major. Fog is bad, staying as left as I can; also raining. I'm just happy to get the heck out of Jacksonville. We parked on the side of the road in front of some people's driveway. Country folk came out wondering what we were doing. Once I told them about the Wounded Warrior Project, they brought out the whole family, the grandmother, brothers, nieces, and grandkids, to wish me luck. Let's thank all the wounded warriors for their service. And give me the strength to get through the day. Blister is pretty bad. But compared to what those guys went through, I think I can handle it.*

When walking down a desolate road, I came across a one-way small bridge. I was very hesitant about walking across it. If a car came across from the other direction at a high speed, or any speed for that matter, I was toast. I would have no room to maneuver unless I jumped off into the river. Unfortunately, I do not know how to swim!

I know what you're thinking. You're a graduate of the United

States Merchant Marine Academy. Don't you have to pass a swim test to graduate?

Yes, but I have the sole distinction of being the only graduate of the USMMA who's not able to swim. How? I'm really not very proud of this.

The second day at the academy, my company was sent down to the outside pool for a recess break. The officer in charge told my fellow midshipmen in my company and me to jump into the pool. They all did except me!

The officer came up to me and said, "Mister, did you hear me? Get into the pool."

I just stood there.

He repeated his command in a louder, stern voice.

I finally told him in an embarrassed tone that I did not know how to swim. Consequently, I was assigned during my limited free time as a plebe (freshman) to take swimming lessons.

After several months of these classes, three of my fellow non-swimming classmates had passed their swimming tests. This test consisted of swimming four laps of the pool and treading water for five minutes. I had managed to talk to my instructor, a very nice man with Italian ancestry, and get him to accept the four lap requirement swimming on my back. He anxiously wanted the class to end so he would have a free class period. However, I could not tread water for my life (play on words here!).

My instructor was getting impatient. During these months taking swim lessons, my mother (a great Italian cook) would send care packages, which included a variety of great Italian delicacies. I would always save a few Italian treats for my swim instructor, who just devoured them. Finally, I had my mother bake a whole pan of lasagna with meatballs. I gave it to my instructor at our next swim class. At the end of that class, he informed me that he was passing me. God works in mysterious ways!

Unfortunately, I still do not know how to swim. In my defense, I made sure all my three children learned how to swim.

Back to my walk. I called my big brother Mikey. Together we planned for him to drive across the bridge, make a U-turn, and drive back to the end of the bridge. Mikey's car would effectively block access to the bridge. I was still a little nervous about this.

At that moment a police car came down the road and stopped. He approached me. I explained to him about my walk. He put his lights on and allowed me to walk behind his car across the bridge. I was so thankful. I rewarded the officer with a Wounded Warrior Bracelet and a big heartfelt thank you. Bridges would soon become a real big issue for me, a life-and-death issue!

## Day 21—Mileage Walked: 15.52 (Kingsland, Georgia)

*Walking through the blister and a few miles will put me in Georgia. Three weeks on the road. Hopefully this time next week, I will be walking into Savannah, Georgia, which will be really, really major. I'm right on schedule if all goes right in the next couple of days. That's really good, considering the rain day I lost, the day with the Wounded Warrior Project, the time with the TV morning show, and yesterday with my blister. Okay, so I can crank seventeen today, and hopefully the rain will stay off. Okay, God be with me.*

# Day 22, Week 4—No Audio, Mileage Walked: 14.98 (Kingsland, Georgia)

Getting back to Mikey. I was so appreciative of my brother being my support driver. This adventure was so totally out of his element. I remember approaching a small convenience store located in a rural area as I finished my morning mileage. I saw Mikey standing in front of the store. It was lunchtime. I said, "Mikey, why don't you go in and pick up lunch for us?"

He told me he was not going into that place alone. He was scared because the small supermarket was not situated in the best of locations.

I laughed and called him a *gatto spaventoso*, which in Italian means a scaredy-cat. We went into the store together.

My brother asked the counter clerk if they had any sandwiches.

She gave him a quizzical look. She then proceeded to call for the manager of the store.

The manager came out from the back.

My brother asked if they had any sandwiches.

The manager hesitated with a quizzical look. The manager told us he would go look in the back freezer. A few minutes later, he came out and stated, "No, we have none of those sandwich things."

I looked at my brother. It was one of the few times I have seen Mikey truly speechless. So we left the store with a lot of junk stuff, a bag of ice, and water. I started to soak my feet. Mikey went on and on about how could they not know what a sandwich was. I told him that he wasn't in Kansas anymore!

As a sidebar to this, he did stop another day at a store in the middle of nowhere. Well, the owner of the store was of Italian heritage and from New Jersey, our hometown state. My brother was in his glory. He had someone to throw the bull with. When he came to drop off my food and ice at lunchtime, he told me about this encounter. The hero sandwiches were free. He handed me the phone number of the person from the store for me to call him. I called and thanked him. We reminisced about New Jersey for a while. The hero sandwich was great. Mikey still had food dripping on his face from his Italian hero! Priceless!

# Day 23—Mileage Walked: 14.57 (Brunswick, Georgia)

*It was raining like heck. So we started two hours later. At least it stopped and is now just drizzling. About 110 miles outside of Savannah, going north on Routes 17 and 25, passing a lot of deteriorated old homes. It's funny: one house had a lock on the front door, but half of the front door was gone. Pretty funny looking.*

*Not too much traffic, which makes it good. Catching up on things; pretty much getting back to normal. That's good to know. Michael has two more days. I think he can't wait to get back. Nick will be down then. So look forward to that. Hopefully the rain will stay away. My blister doesn't hurt too badly. Maybe get at least fifteen miles, but it's getting dark. See what we can do.*

# Day 24—Mileage Walked: 17.32
# (Country Club Estates, Georgia)

*I guess this is one of the bumps in the road. I have been sitting here for an hour waiting for my brother, who can't decide whether I'm north or south from him. He can't find the only large bridge that exits on Route 17 that runs into Brunswick. So in the world of GPS, phones, and common sense, it all seems to be in cyberspace for him. I'm hoping he can find me. I'm having to skip lunch now and hopefully get the other eight miles in. Should have tried to walk across the bridge. Okay, hopefully he will find me in the next millennium!*

I'm shivering on the side of the road. With all the walking I was doing, even on a cold day, my shirt would become soaked through with sweat. So once I stopped walking, my body temperature would really drop. Sitting down on this cold, windy day after walking my ten miles, soaked with perspiration, I was starting to shake and getting very concerned because Mikey had not shown up yet.

Across from me was a huge bridge, which could be seen for miles in any direction. Where the heck was Mikey? Finally, he arrived one hour late. I opened the car door and looked at Mikey. He saw my look. He said he was just following his GPS! I was starting to firmly believe he used his GPS to get from his bed to the bathroom at night.

That same day, early evening, when Mikey came to pick me up, he said it would be an hour to get back to the hotel. I said in my head this couldn't be right.

Mikey said, "Look at the GPS!"

So I called my friend Nick. I told him where we were. I asked him to google directions back to the hotel for me. He responded back shortly. We were only fifteen minutes from the hotel. As we headed back to the hotel, Mikey told me the GPS in his car only worked on highway tracking. After freezing, no lunch, and behind today's schedule, I just looked at Mikey and said, "Okay." Luckily he's my brother, or I would be in prison for what I was thinking about doing to him.

As soon as we got back to the hotel, I said, "Let me take care of my feet and let's get something to eat at Outback."

So a little while later, Mikey and I hopped into his car. Guess what? Mikey told me the Outback's address was plugged into his GPS and we were only about thirty-five minutes away.

So I said, "Okay, let's go; I'm hungry." Later, after filling my belly and actually having a drink, we left the Outback Restaurant.

The cars exiting out of the restaurant parking lot were backed up. I said, "Mikey, let's drive around the other side and see if we can get out the back way. It's getting late."

So we drove around the other side of the building. What's on the other side of the street? *Our hotel!* I just looked at Mikey and started to laugh. I said I was going to rip out his GPS and dump it out the window. For the second time in his life, Mikey had no words.

I remember one last thing about Mikey's final day being my support driver. He picked me up on time with my lunch. I stepped into the car.

He looked at me and said, "Boy, am I tired."

I looked at him. "You're tired? Try walking fifteen miles in a morning! In fact, just go walk one mile and let me know how it feels!"

I was truly appreciative of Mikey driving me for ten days. For him, this was as difficult as it was for me to do my walk. So having said that, I will always be in Mikey's debt. Mikey's GPS is another story!

# Day 25—No Audio, Mileage Walked: 16.15 (En Route to Midway, Georgia)

**Interlude 3**

Sometimes being a brother is even better than being a superhero.
—Marc Brown

## Mikey

Earlier I gave you some insight into Mikey. It was probably the hardest job for him to be one of my support drivers for several different reasons. I truly was thankful and respected Mikey for hanging in with me for ten days. When we decided he would leave early in the morning on my off day and not wait for Nick to show up, I never saw anybody move so fast. It was like a gale wind behind him as he hustled down the hotel corridor to leave. I just started laughing watching him haul his butt out of the hotel.

As a side note, Mikey tore his Achilles tendon right before I arrived at Yankee Stadium. He was not able to fly up to see the conclusion of my walk. I felt very bad about this. Truth be known, most of my family for various reasons were not in attendance at Yankee Stadium when I touched home plate. I wasn't disappointed. I was just sad. However, my children, my nephew Andy, Gary's son, Ari, his wife, and several of my dearest friends were there. I was so blessed!

An excerpt from Mikey's interview on his last day follows.

*The most surprising thing was the amount of work. It was more than driving a car. You had to know what city you were in, what road you were on, and where you could get a good hero. Well, like I said, he is my brother, and I have been with him for sixty-four years, and there is not too much I don't know about him. What impressed me was his get-up-and-go, whatever the weather; whether it was rain, warm, snow, he did what he had to do. I hope God continues to bless him in his trip and look forward to seeing him in Yankee Stadium.*

## Chapter 10

# SAVANNAH

Never fear shadows. They simply mean there's
a light shining somewhere nearby.
—Ruth Renkel

Nick, whom I have known since the fifth grade, was my next support driver. Nick flew to Savannah at his own expense to meet up with me. I rented a car to be available to him once he arrived at the airport. Nick met me at my hotel. Mikey had left that morning. I knew how difficult it was for Mikey being my support driver. Luckily we loved each other so much. Otherwise, I truly would have strangled him. With his GPS episodes, jokes about me getting run over on the road, how tired he was each day, and the stress of my walk, it was time to begin a new chapter less Mikey. Having said this, I love him dearly.

### Day 26—Mileage Walked: 16.87 (Midway, Georgia)

*Approximately forty-five miles to the outside of Savannah. Not too bad a day; the traffic is good. The bugs are horrible. It's unbelievable how these bugs find you and want to eat you up. It's really crazy. Thank God the bug spray is working somewhat. Okay, my feet are feeling pretty good. Hopefully will be able to knock the ten miles off this morning. Nick has been really great, no worries or anything. All right, God protect me.*

### Day 27—No Audio, Mileage Walked: 15.58 (Location: Midway, Georgia)

# Day 28—Rest Day, Mileage Walked: 0

*Well, yesterday was the closest I came to being killed. It was more than very scary. I was walking on the road when I heard a* whoosh. *I looked to my right. It was like sitting in your car and the other car is so close to your side window that you could reach out and touch it. The car came by with such force it blew me forward and propelled me off my feet. I could not believe the idiot had passed the car in the other lane and came over into my lane. I was pretty shook up. It really made me aware of the dangers of this trip. Also, thank God for keeping me alive and wanting me to get back to my kids. I guess the cards are not in my hand to play, but it was very, very scary.*

*Very fortunately, a few minutes later, a law enforcement deputy sheriff came by. He said he saw me in the world news yesterday. I told him about the incident. I didn't get the car license number. I just can't understand how people can take those kinds of risks with people's lives. I pray God keeps me safe for the rest of my voyage.*

*Leaving today for Savannah. Should be right on the outskirts by the end of today. Tomorrow is Sunday. An off day and will be four weeks on the trip. One-third done—amazing. Mentally a few chips short, but for the most part, hanging strong. Okay, God be with me.*

*An excerpt from the conversation with the deputy sheriff follows:*
Me: *What's your name?*
Porter: *Grant Porter.*
Me: *Grant Porter just stopped by, even though he is a Braves fan and I'm a Yankees fan.*
Porter: *I remember the '96 and '99 World Series. It's very difficult giving a Yankee fan some money, but considering the Wounded Warrior Project, very well worth it.*
Me: *Thank you; very much appreciated.*
Porter: *Wish I had been here earlier to help you out.*
Me: *I wish you were too. A very close call, a very close call.*
*All right, just getting ready to start, freezing my butt off, but I'm off tomorrow. Nick, my support driver, is dropping me exactly where I was yesterday. I will be in a suburb of Savannah, Richmond Hill. Tomorrow I'm going to stay in bed and rest my tootsies.*

Nick and I were getting ready to go out for dinner. At the front desk of the hotel, we asked the clerk if he could recommend any good Italian restaurants. He handed us a flyer on a local restaurant. We had difficulty locating it. Finally, after driving around in circles awhile, I called the restaurant for directions. A woman answered my call. I asked if she could give us the address and possibly directions. After a slight hesitation on the phone, she responded she didn't know the address or where she could find it. I told her that she should go outside and look on the wall by the door and read me the numbers. She agreed. At that same moment I saw the restaurant ahead of us. We saw the waitress walking out and looking at the wall. I looked at Nick, shaking my head. Welcome to rural America.

We parked the car and greeted the waitress as we walked into the establishment. Shortly after we sat down, she took our order. I asked if the veal was real veal. She responded that there was no sign on it saying it was not real. I waited a few seconds to digest her words and proceeded to order my food, which included a side order of broccoli.

Shortly after, she brought out my food. There were some green stems on the side. I asked, "What is that?"

She responded, "Broccoli."

I asked, "Did you see anything else next to it on the counter in the kitchen that might have been bushy green?"

She looked confused and said, "No."

Nick and I surmised that when she went back to get our order, the chef (I use this term lightly) had cut off the stems to the head of the broccoli and left them on the counter. The waitress must have assumed this was the broccoli and brought it out to us.

During our meal I thanked her for trying to give us the address of the place. She said no problem and thanked me for letting her know where she could locate the address from now on. She then asked if I wanted more tea. I said that would be great. She returned to our table with hot water, reached into my teacup and pulled out the tea bag, squeezed it with her hands into my cup, and then replaced it with another tea bag! I just looked at Nick.

I won't comment on the veal. I made a mistake when I asked if it was real veal. I should have asked if it was really meat! This was sad and yet comical after my exhausting walk from the day. However, we did leave a very nice tip.

## Day 29, Week 5—Mileage Walked: 15.45 (Richmond Hill and Garden City, Georgia)

*Four weeks already in. Coming up on Savannah. Took a tour yesterday. It was my day off, but I fell asleep. Actually slept till five thirty in the morning. What a bonus! Fighting off a cold. Blister getting better. I should be in South Carolina tomorrow. Keeping my head on straight, staying positive, keeping all the negatives out. Wish me a good day. God be with me.*

Walking through Savannah, I remember coming across a concrete pillar with an inscription on it. The inscription read as follows:

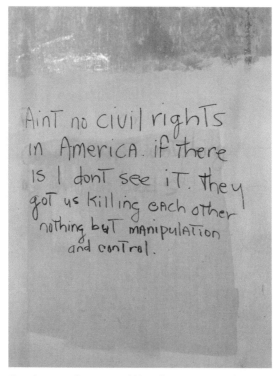

*Handwritten sign on pillar in Savannah, Georgia.*

## Day 30—Mileage Walked: 16.35 (Savannah, Georgia)

*Leaving Savannah; will be in South Carolina shortly. Don't want to be negative, but people were not very friendly here. I must have said hello to at least five different people of all different races. No response back.*

*Just not very outward. Don't want to judge them, but not very friendly is the best way I can put it. Today is Tuesday. In six days hopefully will be in Charleston. Nick is hanging in good. Did another radio interview from Florida. So feel pretty good. See how I am after today. Hoping the roads will be better on the South Carolina side. I will be on 17a and then 170 going through a small little town. Going up to Buford and then Charleston. Okay, God keep me safe.*

## Day 31—Mileage Walked: 15.91
## (Hardeeville, South Carolina)

*April 1, the first day of the month, month number 2, one-third down. After yesterday's horrendous day dodging bullets on Route 17, hopefully will have smooth sailing. Having a private walk (just the trees and me) here for a few miles. It's like walking in heaven. All right, God be with me.*

*South Carolinians are just like Georgians. They just mind their own business. They don't come up to you asking about the walk to New York. They just don't say poop. Just let you walk by. Not like New Yorkers. They just mind their own business. I guess that's what makes this country great. Everybody has their own way.*

## Day 32—Mileage Walked: 12.86
## (Shell Point, South Carolina)

*Hey, sidewalks, sidewalks, I'm excited! A good day when you have side-walks, room on the side to walk and not much traffic. It's amazing the small things that get you excited. Today is day 32, Thursday, April 2. Coming into Buford on my way to Charleston. Nick is hanging in. Bill is coming in Sunday. So hopefully a month from now, I will be in Richmond on the homeward stretch. Having a few weak moments but reaching down, looking at my soul, and hoping it's still there. All right, God, talk to you soon.*

*Okay, I'm out of Buford and walking on Route 21. Started to walk across a bridge with no room on the side.* Maybe I will risk it. *Just got to that point when a truck came over and blew me sideways. I said, "Second thought, I'm calling Nicky. I think that's it for tonight. No sense risking it."*

## Day 33—Mileage Walked: 15.99 (Laurel Bay, South Carolina)

*Still heading toward Charleston; it's Good Friday. Getting my massage tonight. Can't wait! Lots of sidewalks for a little while, I hope. Still playing the mental game. I can do this. Okay, here we go.*

## Day 34—Mileage Walked: 14.44 (En Route to Ravenel, South Carolina)

*Approximately thirty-nine miles outside of Charleston. Got up this morning and said, "No way I'm going to be able to walk today. Blisters are really starting to hurt." But I'm here. Might get some rain today. I never thought I'd get out, but I'm pretty tough. All right, hopefully the traffic will be slim pickings. Okay, day 34.*

*Just had lunch at Flo's Diner. Southern fried chicken, ham in the green beans, and also cherry pie, banana pudding. Really was great. Our waitress was so sweet.*

We left our waitress a very nice tip. She seemed surprised we left a tip. Everything in the place was so authentic, all the homemade pies and the waitresses with their aprons on.

One day, not necessary to mention the town, but as I was walking through it, I had to ask people for some directions. Swear to God, every one of them had only one visible tooth. I distinctly remember asking a young couple sitting on a swing set for directions. They both smiled at me. One tooth in each mouth! In one way it was comical; in another way very sad. I don't know if the town had a severe drug issue with the use of speed, ice, or meth!

That evening Nick and I stopped in the same town at a local drugstore for some supplies. As I stood at the counter looking at the prescriptions in the alphabetically arranged slots, I noticed a side wall approximately eight feet high adjacent to it and stacked with prescriptions about four feet high. I called Nicky over to let him see it. Pointing, I said, "Nick, there's at least ten prescriptions there for each person in this small town." That was a real eye-opener for both of us.

## Day 35—Rest Day, Mileage Walked: 0

## Day 36, Week 6—No Audio, Mileage Walked: 16.08 (Ravenel, South Carolina)

## Day 37—No Audio, Mileage Walked: Not Recorded (Shell Point and Mount Pleasant, Georgia)

## Day 38—Mileage Walked: 16.37 (En Route to Georgetown, South Carolina)

*Getting closer and closer to the halfway mark. Like to say I remember the town I'm in—oh, Mount Pleasant, South Carolina, on 17 heading for Georgetown. Fortunately on a bypass road that has sidewalks. The weather looks decent. So looking to get back into the groove. Bill is working out well for me. And he is so meticulous with all the mileage calculations. His mind is so scientifically oriented. It's really great. All right, talk to you later.*

My first fanny pack, which included phone charger, tape recorder, first aid equipment, suntan spray, card holder, headphones, plastic rain jacket, mace, and toilet paper finally broke apart. I went to the store and purchased a duplicate one the same color. For the first few days using the new fanny pack, I felt like I had lost a personal connection. I refused to throw away my original fanny pack. We had gone through so much together. Rain and life-and-death situations were only a few instances. However, after a week, I finally decided to discard it. I was carrying enough gear already. Actually thought about burying it! My mind was getting a little nutso with all the walking wearing on my head.

## Day 39—No Audio, Mileage Walked: 16.23 (Georgia)

## Day 40—Mileage Walked: 16.13 (En Route to Georgetown, South Carolina)

*Yes, I'm in the forties. Five days away from the midpoint. Still a little breezy. Still on Route 17 heading toward Georgetown. Will be there to-morrow. Hotel is nice. I was thankful to get out of parts of Charleston that were real rattraps. So it's going pretty good. The traffic isn't that bad.*

*Morning show blew me off. Not a real big thing in the realm of things. So keeping strong, mentally getting more difficult, but God is with me. I know I can do it. So let's do it.*

## Day 41—No Audio, Mileage Walked: 13.26 (Georgetown, South Carolina)

## Day 42—Mileage Walked: 16.76 (Georgetown and Murrells Inlet, South Carolina)

*Week 6 completed. Halfway mark as far as weeks. On my way to Myrtle Beach. Things going pretty good with Bill. Still going to be short a driver, but not going to worry about it. I also need to get my act together. Thinking about the good and get off the negatives. It would be nice not to have this little toe hurting. It is what it is! Myrtle Beach and then off to North Carolina. All right! Wonder if everybody is with me.*

*Went to town last night. Italian restaurant had the best frutti di mare ever. A beautiful waitress named Montana was our server. She is going to be a dental assistant. She was very nice. Really excellent—a small little place, already in my mind scrabbling to remember the name of it. I know it started with an A [laughing to myself] at least. Had an ice cream, splurge, I think I deserved it.*

*Today looks like a beautiful day again. Day 42, starting with a positive mind. See how everything works out.*

Wish I could remember the exact spot of that restaurant. It was on my way to Charleston.

**Interlude 4**

> It is one of the blessings of old friends that you
> can afford to be stupid with them.
> —Ralph Waldo Emerson

**Nick**

I met Nick in the fifth grade. I immediately gave him the nickname "Paisano," which translates to compatriot. For me, it translated to best friend. Nick is such a giving person. If you stopped him on the street and asked him for anything, if it was in his power, he would give it to you. Many times I would tell him people were taking advantage of him. He would just smile at me.

One time Nick helped me out with a substantial loan. When I was finally able to pay it back, he wouldn't take the money. He said, "Just put it toward your kids' college." I could write a book just on all his good deeds.

One example is at a spring training game in Dunedin watching the Yankees play the Blue Jays. Nick won the fifty-fifty raffle. I accompanied him to collect the money. The raffle was sponsored by the Girl Scouts. Nick won $800. He showed his ticket and immediately said, "Keep the money for the Girl Scouts." I should point out Nick wasn't wealthy. That was Nick! If I was ever in a foxhole, Nick would be the first person I would want with me.

An excerpt from Nick's interview on his last day follows:

*What surprised me the most was the amount of distance you covered. A lot! I felt a lot of pressure doing my job. There was a lot of behind-the-scenes stuff you had to do. That you get up at 4:30 a.m., doing your routine, making your power drink, whatever the heck it is, doing your exercise, Epsom salts soak, computer work, a lot of work, preventive stuff—it was not just the walk; it's a lot of preparation you have to deal with. It's a lot of work on your part, Rich, I gotta say!*

*Chapter 11*

# THE ART OF PEEING ON THE ROAD, TRUCKS, AND DOGS!

What most people tend to forget
Is that we have unbelievable control
Over our destiny.
—Bill Gove

A delicate topic indeed! For those readers who might not be totally up to speed, restrooms don't exist on every road in the United States! When walking down a road in the country, it is not a big issue for a man to unzip his fly and urinate. However, walking into the woods can be an issue. For example, I was getting picked up after my day's walk. Before getting into the car, I walked across a ditch into the woods and quickly urinated. No problem. The next day, I was dropped off at the same location to start my morning walking. Having to urinate before starting, I again went to walk across the same ditch, only it must have rained and flooded the night before. As I walked across the ditch, I suddenly sank into the mud up to my knees. It was like quicksand. Fortunately, I was still wearing my moccasins, not my good walking sneakers.

Another time, my support driver Bill had dropped me off in front of a deserted, dilapidated gas station. It was located on an old farm road. I walked around back. I saw a cluster of trees. I walked into the middle of the trees and began to pull my pants down. As I was doing this, I noticed an opening in the trees. I could see a sign posted on a nearby tree: "Beware of Dog." Immediately after reading the sign, I heard barking. I had grown up with Saint Bernard dogs all my life, so I didn't have a fear of dogs regardless of size. Let me tell you, whatever kind of dog this animal was, it was intent on changing my philosophy of trusting dogs. There's nothing more unfriendly than a dog growling with a southern accent!

I immediately pulled up my pants and started racing for the front of the gas station building, yelling to Bill at the same time to open the car door. He must have seen me in his mirror and the rhinoceros-size dog chasing me. I dove into the car and closed the door just before the dog crashed into it.

I always check for snakes and poison ivy every time I enter the woods to go to the bathroom. Thank God I never ran across any snakes. Poison ivy was another story. I'm embarrassed to say, one day while walking down a rural road with nice homes and manicured front yards, nature called very quickly. Literally there was no place to do my business. I spotted one house with some nice bushes in a circular formation in the front yard. I went into the middle of the flower bed and ducked low. Thank God that I always carried toilet paper in my backpack.

When walking through cities, I found that a lot of places would not allow you to use their facilities. In some cases, you would not want to use their facilities! So I became adept at walking down side streets between alleys or behind cars. I always had two fears. One was getting caught urinating in a city block and, two, getting caught by law enforcement and consequently getting booked for public indecency. I just thought, how would I explain that to the Wounded Warrior Project organization? On a side note, I always made sure my support driver informed me where schools were located. With everything going on in the world, I did not want to get anywhere close to a school when I needed to relieve myself.

Another fear was relieving myself on one of these side farm roads, hitting an electrified fence, and getting lit up like a Christmas tree! Toward the end of the trip, running out of steam, I did not want to waste any vital energy trying to find a good place to go to the bathroom. My next-to-last day, totally ready to complete my journey, I was on my lunch break in urban Fort Lee, New Jersey, with Jimmy as my support driver. Jimmy was doing the last leg with me.

I was so tired and beat up, I just opened the passenger door, stood up, and peed behind the door. Well, Jimmy, who is very conservative, started going nuts. "Are you crazy? There's a girl on the other side of the road." I looked up. The girl was at least a quarter mile up the other side of the street. I told Jimmy I was not that endowed for her to see anything, plus the door was covering me. You would have thought I robbed a bank by his reaction. At that point, I was nearing the end of the road and my patience.

One more dog story to share. As I was walking down a country road (wish I had a tally of how many country routes I walked on!) and heard some barking, loud barking. Focusing my eyes on where the barking was coming from, I noticed three large, did I say large, Saint Bernard-type large dogs. As I walked closer, I noticed the first two had heavy chains restraining them, but the third dog did not. I wasn't nervous because there was a three-foot ditch with water flowing at a good pace separating their location from the road. I figured, no problem and continued to walk past them on the other side of the moat! They were barking like crazy.

As I walked past them, the third, unchained dog started running toward me. This was no problem. Heck, I had a minimoat between us! As I said, I raised Saint Bernards and was used to big dogs. The dogs were on the other side of a wide ditch. What could go wrong? Well, was I in for a surprise! The unleashed dog just vaulted over the ditch and came running right for me. I turned. I carried mace with me, but I really didn't want to use it on the dog. Yet I did not want to become this dog's lunch.

For some reason, Saint Francis must have slapped me beside the head. I recalled a time when I had two Saint Bernards, Bonnie and Clyde. Now Clyde weighed 220 pounds plus. One day Clyde saw an old man walking down the street by my home. He ran off the property, which he'd never done before, and started running after the old man. I'm laughing as I write this because what I'm calling an old man was probably around sixty. Today at my age of sixty-eight, I would really get mad at somebody referring to me as an old man. It's funny how your perspective changes in time. Well, getting back to Clyde chasing the old man. The old man heard Clyde barking behind him, turned around, and immediately in a very authoritative voice yelled at Clyde to stop. Well, Clyde, to my surprise, stopped and sat. The old man just continued walking down the street.

So, recalling this story, as the dog started galloping toward me with open mouth, teeth glaring, and drool spitting, I yelled, "Stop!" in my loudest authoritarian voice while grabbing the mace. To my surprise and relief, the dog just stopped in his tracks. I said, "Good, boy." Then I turned around and started walking slowly. Definitely Saint Francis, patron saint of animals, was with me.

When walking down very isolated roads with high trees on each side, it could become very lonely. Some stretches I felt like I could see ten miles down the road. So every once in a while, I would smell it first, the scent of freshly cut timber, then see a logging truck. The lumber truck drivers all throughout my trip would always give me a big boost. A blast on their horn would be so uplifting. This meant so much to me. When walking for eight hours not seeing anything living and smelling like a pig, getting the whiff of the timber and a friendly wave made my day.

## Day 43, Week 7—No Audio, Mileage Walked: 10.91 (Garden City, South Carolina)

## Day 44—Mileage Walked: 16.06 (Surfside Beach and Myrtle Beach)

*Waiting to see my morning show airing. Hopefully it will come on today. Bill has been a great help. Straightened me out about wasting energy. It's raining out. It will be tough again getting the mileage. But I know I can't beat the weather. It is what it is, so will take it from there.*

*Well, like I said, day 44 (my halfway mark), it finally stopped raining on the trail. Really getting excited because we found a back road in the Myrtle Beach tourist section. I'm just not going to worry about days or support drivers. Whatever is meant to be is meant to be. It will all work out, and the Wounded Warriors will come across by the finish line. I just have my faith in God. So, I'm right down on a nice paved road, and the rain is staying off a little bit. If I can get my mileage in today, I can stay on target hopefully. So less worrying about finances and logistics and more concentrating on what I can get out of this trip. My holy grail!*

While I was walking through Myrtle Beach, a car pulled over next to me. A guy jumped out of the car and asked me if I was the person walking from Tampa to the Bronx. I said, "Yes." He immediately started waving to his car, and two other men got out. David, the man who first jumped out of the car, started yelling, "I told you it was him!" He then explained to me that on TV last night in the hotel, he saw a news bulletin about a guy who robbed a bank and escaped in Myrtle Beach. His brother Rob did not want to stop when he saw me walking because I looked like the bank robber.

Well, once we established that I was not the bank robber, Rob and David asked if they could treat me to breakfast. I said thanks but told them I'd had breakfast a few hours ago. Rob then asked if they could take me to play a round of golf. I started to laugh and said, "Appreciate it, but have to keep walking." I then noticed New Jersey license plates and asked if they were from New Jersey. They responded yes, they were from Bergen County. They wanted to know if I knew where Bergen County was. I laughed some more and informed them I was born in Hackensack, New Jersey, lived my childhood in Washington Township, and went to school at Saint Joseph's Regional in Montvale. They told me their kids went to Bergen Catholic, my old school's archrival. But they had a nephew that went to Saint Joe's.

We agreed to meet for dinner at my hotel that night as I was still going to be in Myrtle Beach. Later, over dinner, we shared information and stories about our childhoods in New Jersey. While talking, I mentioned Westwood and a friend named Al Smith. One of the people at a table across from us yelled, "Hey, I'm from Westwood, and I know Al's brother on the police force." I laughed. What a small world. But it was going to get even smaller.

As I talked to David, I told him how my walk had been jump-started with the help of Andrew Levy. He started to laugh and told me Andrew was one of his good friends. He took out his phone and immediately called Andrew. On the phone, David told Andrew, "You will never guess who I'm having dinner with." He then told him and handed the phone over to me.

I told Andrew, "Can you believe this!" I then told him, "Now we have proof that I'm actually doing the walk. Meeting these guys on the walk will validate it!"

Well, around seven thirty, I started to nod off and almost dropped my head on the table. David said to everybody at the table, "Man, he looks tired. You better get him back to the hotel." But before leaving,

David got my itinerary and told me he was going to send me new walking shoes and some cases of water. I was so grateful, especially when the shoes showed up a week or so later at my hotel.

Little did I know at that time that I would meet David again on the road. He would come to my rescue at the end of my journey.

*Bill and I doing a selfie!*

## Day 45—Mileage Walked: 17.03 (North Myrtle Beach and Little River, South Carolina)

*It's a special day for a couple of reasons. Yesterday was the halfway mark for days of my trip. Tomorrow I will be going over the six-hundred-mile threshold, which will be more than halfway.*

Usually at breakfast someone would notice my walking shirt and come over to say something to me. On this particular morning, a man came over to say hello. He shook my hand with tears in his eyes. He told me that without the support of the Wounded Warrior Project, his brother would be dead. He explained his brother lost all his toes on both feet in Iraq. When he came home, he was suicidal.

He found out about the Wounded Warrior Project. He attended some of their programs. These programs gave him the emotional support he needed. Now he was on the road to recovery. The man shook my hand again and once more stated if it wasn't for the Wounded Warrior Project, his brother would be dead.

Throughout my walk, numerous people came up to me with stories about friends and loved ones whose lives were saved by the support of the Wounded Warrior Project programs. Here is an excerpt from an article written by Robert David Jaffe in the *Huffington Post*:

> *When asked how we as a country should deal with the toll on our troops, who have fought in Iraq and Afghanistan, Albero said that "number one is recognizing that it (the toll) does exist." He pointed out that it is not an isolated phenomenon.*
>
> *No one knows for sure how many veterans have PTSD and TBI among other afflictions, but the number of suicides in our military is quite high by historical standards. As Albero said, "We ignore the large percentage of people that are affected." He added that many of those troops are "young" which he believes makes them even more susceptible to these injuries, some of which are hard to discern or diagnose.*

*Crossing North Carolina state line.*

## Day 46—Mileage Walked: 13.70 (Carolina Shores, North Carolina)

*Hi! Today is a very good day because I crossed over into North Carolina, and tomorrow I will be at the six-hundred-mile mark, which is the halfway mark for my trip, which is looking around twelve hundred miles, so pretty excited. Some days are longer than others. I'm feeling good. I thank you all for keeping me in your thoughts and prayers. As I get closer and closer to New York, I will be able to give you more updates, and hopefully you all will be able to see me shortly crossing home plate at Yankee Stadium. Take care!*

## Day 47—No Audio, Mileage Walked: 17.52 (Shallotte, North Carolina)

## Day 48—Rest Day, Mileage Walked: 2.59 (Wilmington, North Carolina)

*Walking through the heart of Wilmington, North Carolina, Route 17 B. Very nice area. Just met Crystal doing her exercise. Nice young lady originally from the Bronx. Really a small world. My energy level is a lot stronger now that I'm back in the Hampton Inns. Now I just have to find a place to take a leak. Hopefully will be out of Wilmington today and in three days will be in Jacksonville, North Carolina.*

*Yesterday got to see the Yes TV show, which was really good. I have to say I look decent. They had me on the morning show. Dante called with some really kind words.*

One day at the end of my walk, my phone charger went dead. I found a house converted into a store. It seemed like some kind of computer store. I entered and informed the lady working behind the counter about my walk. She allowed me to use her phone charger. It so happened she was originally from New Jersey! As we were talking, I was telling her how bad the bugs were, especially in the morning when doing my stretching and warm-up before starting out. She offered for me to come to her store the next morning to start the walk and stretch there. I was so appreciative. A bug-free-start day! It was these kind acts that helped warm my soul.

During this time I had a meltdown. It was always a hassle finding a hotel room that was not too far either for the morning drop-off or for pickup late in the afternoon. After walking close to twenty miles, the last thing I wanted to do was ride in a car for thirty minutes or more fighting traffic back to my hotel. The other issue was switching hotel rooms almost every night. I tried reserving two if not three days at the same hotel. In this way I could do three days of walking and at most be only sixty miles from my hotel and hopefully a minimum drive back time-wise.

This was the bane of my existence. Well, one night we finally found a hotel in a low-income section of town and close to my next morning drop-off. I had no choice. For whatever reason, I was more tired than usual. After lugging my stuff from the parking lot to my room, which was almost another quarter mile to walk, I had to take a shower. Well, neither the shower nor the toilet worked. Bill got us a different room. We then had to lug our stuff back toward the parking lot into the new room. This room was filthy and with no hot water. Well, I just lost it. I started with a tirade of curse words both in English and Italian. It went on for a good ten minutes. Bill just sat back and observed.

When I was done, he said, "You want to go to another place?"

I said, "Yes," even though it would be a real pain in the neck moving all my stuff again.

I needed this blowup. I was getting bored with the routine, homesick, tired of dealing with the nutjobs on the road trying to run me over. Hotels were not giving me any breaks, and finances were becoming an issue. Everything in my body hurt. I wasn't thinking about quitting; I just needed to blow off steam for all the crap that was happening to me.

Bill was really cool. He asked me if it was out of my system.

I said, "Yes." I added, "You have to admit that place really sucked."

# Day 49—Mileage Walked: 18.17
# (Bayshore, North Carolina)

*Week 7, only five more to go. Walking through Wilmington, North Carolina, with sidewalks, which excites me. Bill is still hanging in there;*

*I'm still hanging in there. His snoring is getting better. I got rained out yesterday. Decided to enjoy the trip more, relaxing a little and not wasting all my energy after my meltdown the other day. My ankle is still bothering me.*

*It looks like financially won't be totally in the hole. So I should have all the support drivers taken care of, which is a miracle. So many things have gone my way. Should just take the time being grateful. Bill bailed me out. Carole (future support driver) happened to be up near Richmond. Getting the Wounded Warrior Project to at least help a little bit. All of these have been blessings. So today have to work on finding my soul a little bit better. All right already, I have to admit I'm a good-looking walker!*

## Afternoon

*A nice couple stopped and offered me water and homemade biscuits, which was really sweet. They said they saw me on TV. I took the water and told them I'd love to eat the biscuits but I'm on a strict diet. Have to watch what I eat.*

*Met another guy. Seeing my shirt, he yelled, "Walking to the Bronx? Hope you make it!"*

*I yelled back, "I will make it!" Always positive, I'm going to do it. Although my feet hurt like hell right now.*

While walking in the early morning on an isolated highway, I came across two children at the end of a dirt driveway. Their eyes almost came out of their heads when they saw me walking up to them on the side of the road. I introduced myself. I asked if they were waiting for the school bus. They said yes. My guess was the older boy was around ten and the little girl about six years old. I took out two Wounded Warrior bracelets and two Wounded Warrior Project logo magnets to give to the youngsters. The little girl put it on her wrist. She was just beaming with delight.

I asked them if they had ever heard of the Wounded Warrior Project. They said no. Now that they had the bracelets, I told them they would have to go online at school and learn about the Wounded Warrior Project and the troops who fought to protect them. They promised me they would. I saw the innocence in their eyes and their excitement over getting the bracelets. Somehow I felt that maybe one or both of them might eventually serve our country after seeing what I was doing and hearing my brief history lesson on wounded warriors.

## Day 50, Week 8—Mileage Walked: 18.06 (Hampstead and Sneads Ferry, North Carolina)

*Hard to believe. Two days out of Jacksonville, North Carolina. I feel like a genie in a bottle. Have to rub me the right way to get your wish. All right, feet are feeling better, and ankle is hanging in there. God knows what's wrong with it. Bill's been great. I actually got a full night's sleep last night. He slept in the bathtub, I think. He's so considerate.*

*Kind of enjoying more of the walk and looking at the scenery rather than just a thing to get over with. Maybe that little African American girl I met and gave a bracelet to will grow up to be a doctor and help the wounded warriors. That would be cool. I'm getting to really feel like an ambassador for the wounded warriors. Just wish I weren't so darned tired at night when I go out and meet people. It's hard to be sociable when you're tired. Bill is doing a good job.*

*All right, I have the sun for the first day. Let's see how it goes. All right! Wish me luck.*

*Just passed a work gang. Two guards with big-ass rifles. They made all of them move away from me and go along the tree line. They didn't want them to talk to me whatsoever. Maybe one of them would jump me, change clothes with me real quick. Youser, youser.*

Bill, my support driver, has a real snoring problem. He not only sounds like he is cutting a piece of wood, but the whole forest. I just couldn't sleep at night because of his snoring. It made it very difficult on me walking heavy mileage every day without enough rest. Bill felt very bad about this. He went to the drugstore and spent a lot of money on various snoring devices—pills, tapes, and strips to put across his nose. You name it. Nothing worked. Seeing how bad it was affecting me, he finally started sleeping in the bathtub with the door closed. Is this a kind man or what? One night he went out just to let me get some sleep.

The next morning at breakfast he told me he went to a local club. Some young lady of the night came up to him. Now, Bill is eighty-two. He started conversing with her, telling her about his eight children.

After he finished talking about his children, she told him that was great. She told Bill she had "daddy issues" and felt like they were bonding. At that point, Bill decided to come back to the hotel!

Bill always prided himself on finding shortcuts off the main road for me. He told me about one just off the main highway. When I walked onto it, I saw many military warning signs posted very clearly to keep people out. Great, I was on a military base. The roads were isolated and beautiful. I called Bill to tell him it was a great route, but it was military property. Also, I could hear gunfire off in the distance. I said to Bill I might get shot or arrested.

His response was, "Don't worry." His cavalier attitude made me laugh.

So after about another hour of walking on this military base, I called Bill again. I said, "Bill, I have been arrested for trespassing. They are allowing me this one phone call. The fine is $5,000. Can you come up with the money and bail me out?"

He started yelling back, "I can't believe it!"

Finally, after several minutes, I could not keep the ruse up anymore and told him that I was just kidding. We had a good laugh over it at dinner that night.

## Day 51—Mileage Walked: 17.98
## (Jacksonville, North Carolina)

*Tuesday. I'm heading into Jacksonville, North Carolina. I think I have about sixteen miles to go. I'm on a trail at Camp Lejeune. I don't see any no-trespassing signs. Hopefully nobody will take a shot at me. Just wonderful—don't have to worry about traffic, and there are trees. It's paved so I'm going to try to milk it as far as I can. My ankle is still hurting. C'est la vie.*

*Hope I won't hit another down period physically and mentally with all that Facebook stuff. Early in the morning before breakfast, I update my location, announce future media events, and share some personal recollections. This occupies anywhere from thirty to forty-five minutes of my morning. So I'm taking tomorrow off. Not going to skip my rest day this week.*

*Still shooting for a May 2 Richmond arrival. That will be really great.*

*I will be really excited when I'm heading toward Richmond. So I'm in the fifties as far as days go. It will be really a hoot if I can finish up in seventy-five. That's about all that's new.*

*Missing everybody. Trying to stay strong. All right!*

## Day 52—Rest Day, Mileage Walked: 0

## Day 53—No Audio, Mileage Walked: 18.24 (Pumpkin Center, North Carolina)

*I took yesterday off. It was a good day. Caught up with all the little stuff. Think I'm coming down with a cold. Another crash day. So everything worked out pretty well. Had a meatball hero. Closest thing to New York. Picked up all my pharmacy stuff. Generally a good day. Cramping up a lot, so I got salt tablets, which really help out. On my way to New Bern, where I look forward to soaking my feet in a hot tub. Two-day trip, now hitting the hump period. Okay, I just have to hang tough.*

*Well, I'm in Maysville, North Carolina. I'm passing Pop's Main Street Diner. I guess this is what they call the Deep South. I almost got run over. This guy came across the white line, saw me, and started driving right at me. I jumped into the ditch. Thank goodness. Crazy people out there. He wasn't on the phone. It was like he was in a trance.*

*I hit some sidewalks. In some ways it's like Westwood, maybe seventy-five years ago. Unbelievable. All right, I've got a little over five and a half miles to go. Feeling pretty strong. Goodbye.*

## Day 54—Mileage Walked: 18.06 (Pollocksville, North Carolina)

*It's Friday, and I'm walking through Pollocksville. Yesterday was Maysville, a real slice of America; heading toward New Bern, the quest goes on. Trying to keep mentally strong and a little bit tough. Still haven't had a day where my feet weren't hurting. Hit seven hundred miles today; that's a biggie. All right, talk to you again tomorrow, buddy [myself].*

## Day 55—No Audio, Mileage Walked: 18.02 (New Bern, North Carolina)

My fingers were really starting to become an issue. They just continued to cramp up. When holding a food utensil, I would drop it, which meant I couldn't put food in my mouth. When this cramping happened, I looked like some arthritic monster with gnarly hands. I tried walking with my fingers straight up in the air for a few minutes at a time. Finally, after I started taking salt tablets, the cramping became less of an issue.

It was pretty remarkable that at the age of sixty-five, I did not have any real physical issues. I just had that one bad blister, which forced me to stop one afternoon when it burst. I have a souvenir picture of that bad boy. I don't believe it would pass censorship if I tried to include a picture of it in this book. But other than two days of getting rained out, I never missed a day. Not bad for an old man!

During my walk, Andrew Levy arranged for me to receive a call from George Martin, a former famous New York Giants football player. George had walked across the United States in 2008. While I was walking, George called. I had a whole host of questions for him. He was so kind and came across not like a jock, but. rather as a very well-spoken, educated man. I was so impressed. I could talk very frankly with him about what I was feeling. I had many questions for him about what was in store for me, as the end of my journey was in sight. I felt we shared a bond. We were doing these journeys not for the glory, but to do some good for people.

I have to admit I felt very fortunate when he told me he had missed about a week because of food poisoning. If a professional football athlete had to miss a week, I, a sixty-five-year-old man, was doing "damned good" only missing one afternoon because of injury. For George to take time out of his busy schedule to talk to me was not forgotten. I plan on sending him a copy of this book.

## Day 56—Mileage Walked: 11.23 (Washington, North Carolina)

*My eighth week, definitely closing the gap. This is hump week. If I get through the next seven days, I will be in Richmond. And I'll smell the finish line.*

*Starting to rain. Bill said, "Starting to see what you're made of." Well, I don't know. I don't see what I'm made of. Hopefully at the end of the trip, I will. A big-ass truck is barreling down on me, but things are going well. Not even seven thirty, and we are here. I can't deny it. Another week with Bill, and then he will be heading out. Boy, he was a godsend. All right, God keep me safe today.*

## Day 57, Week 9—Mileage Walked: 18.29 (Williamston, North Carolina)

*Well, my phone went dead, and I didn't realize it. Of course my charger is dead. So I walked into Aaron's electronics and furniture store. Two nice ladies there helped me out. So I called Bill, who I hope will find me. Sent a picture to Facebook. So see how it plays out. So Bill came and got me. I have a shot at nineteen miles today. It is what it is.*

## Day 58—Mileage Walked: 17.83 (Windsor, North Carolina)

*Tuesday. I don't even know where I left off. Oh! Williamston, North Carolina, heading to Elizabeth City. Last big stop before Virginia. My head is not working. Bill brought me chicken soup and Chinese, which really hit the spot. Going for nineteen miles. Tomorrow, I'm off. Well, I have to walk this morning and catch up about nine miles. Finances getting low, but not going to worry about it. We'll see how it all plays out.*

*Should get pretty crazy once I get to Richmond. I just have to hang in here for the next couple of days. Will be something when I get there. It will be a change without Bill around, that's for sure. He has been really great.*

*All right, the clouds here are like someone just put them into the sky, so nice looking. They don't move at all. All right.*

# Day 59—Mileage Walked: 9.16 Miles in the Morning, Afternoon Mileage Not Recorded (En Route to Edenton, North Carolina)

*Okay, warm day. Tomorrow will be two months. Unbelievable! Call me nuts. But Saint Francis is on my left arm. Every time when I see a dog, I ask him to calm them now. Like an aura comes over them. They just calm down. Just like yesterday when I saw that horse in the field. He came running over to me. Let me pet him. It's unbelievable. Like a soul in there. I know you guys think I'm losing it.*

*All right, today should be a rest day, but I have to catch up on eight miles. Will walk four days towards Elizabeth City. Sunday I should hit the Virginia line. A major milestone if I keep my head straight and not worry about everything. All right, let's see what today's adventures hold.*

# Day 60—Rest Day, Mileage Walked: 0 (Edenton, North Carolina)

*Tough to get going this morning. It's raining. I'm in Edenton; very pretty. All statues are of Confederates. Nobody said hello. I will take New Yorkers anytime. Houses are really nice, though. Just absolutely beautiful. Go back to the 1820s. Hopefully can stay out of the rain. Bill's still being a drill sergeant.*

*Today is day 60. Two months. Two-thirds done. Twenty-four more days to go. Doesn't look like anything's going to be happening. I just want to touch home plate and get out of there and get on a plane and head home and start another sector of my life.*

*All right, hopefully the rain stays off, and I get my nineteen miles in today.*

# Day 61—Mileage Walked: 10.52 (Elizabeth City, North Carolina)

*Friday, heading toward Virginia. Still have to catch a leg in Endicott. Raining, raining, pouring, but not raining on me. Don't want to explain that one. All right, also just crossed a bridge. Said my usual Hail Mary and offered a Glory Be up to people who might be walking across a bridge to commit suicide. Maybe that prayer will give them a second thought. All right, give me the strength. All right, I have it.*

*Miserable today. It's raining, wind hollering again, and my feet are wet. Why am I doing this again? A lady just crossed the white line, wanted to make me a permanent part of her hood. Bill would say it's not about you, it's all ego. Hopefully will remember days like this when I get the sunshine.*

## Day 62—Mileage Walked: 22.74
## (En Route to Moyock, North Carolina)

*Well, it's not raining. Hallelujah, and the sun is out. Okay, tomorrow will cross the Virginia line. Unbelievable. It will be May 3. So I have twenty-one days left after tomorrow, which will be three more weeks. Hopefully Monday will be sitting on my butt in Richmond. Which will be really nice to be doing. Looking forward to it. Back to the nineteen miles a day grind. Bill will be leaving Monday. Going to miss him. Unbelievable at the job he did. Even including the snoring [laughing]. All right, I got Chris and Francis with me. Hopefully it will be a good day, a strong day.*

Yesterday, I almost got blown over. The wind was really gusting. I couldn't even walk next to the road it was blowing so hard. I was really afraid the wind was going to blow me into traffic. A truck passed by me at full speed just as the wind was blowing across my face. The wind literally blew me sideways off my feet, throwing me into a culvert. It was a crazy experience, one that I never had experienced before on my walk. It would happen again. That time I was talking to my sister, Rose Ann, while walking across a bridge. A speeding truck came by, leaving me very little space on the side of the bridge. I almost was thrown off the bridge.

It's funny now recalling that particular day. I was walking on a two-lane parkway divided by huge trees, where you could not see the other two lanes. I crossed over a little bridge with hardly any space on its side. A rapidly running water body was on the side of it. As you read above, I was almost blown over by a truck speeding at least seventy miles per hour. I'd been walking sideways, not paying attention because I was on the phone. Well, after almost getting blown over, I still remember my thoughts afterward. Jeez, if I get blown over into this water (remember I can't swim!), would I just drift away somewhere? They would never have found my body. Everything would have been for naught. All of this because I was talking on my phone.

The day before, with my head down, reading something while walking through the Hampton Inn's lobby, I fell over a small couch. I was walking full speed ahead. I put my arms out, luckily catching myself without breaking my wrists. Everybody came running over to see if I was okay. It would have been a helluva way to get hurt after all the walking that I had done. It's funny now but not funny when it happened. Just my perspective on how easily something could have gone wrong on this adventure.

## Day 63—Mileage Walked: 17.56 (Elizabeth, North Carolina)

*Nine weeks, unbelievable, catching up the lost miles here in Elizabeth City. In another mile, Bill will pick me up, and we'll head up toward Virginia. Tomorrow, Richmond. Will be only twelve miles from what I need. So doing really, really well. Starting to chill down a little bit, which is good. Got my soul all cleaned out now and starting to put things in there. Had a good night's sleep for the most part, which was a change. So that was good. All right, so the goal is nineteen miles today to be within a hair's breadth of the Virginia line before we head over to Richmond.*

*Crossing into Virginia.*

# Day 64, Week 10—Mileage Not Recorded. (Outside of Moyock, North Carolina)

*Well, I'm about two hundred yards from the Virginia sign on the other side of the road. Which I will be excited to reach. Got tears in my eyes, grabbing my soul, unbelievable. They said I couldn't do it! Three more weeks, may I have the strength to do it and suck it up. All righty, I did it.*

## Interlude 5

Lots of people want to ride with you in the limo, but what you want is someone who will take the bus with you when the limo breaks down.
—Oprah Winfrey

## Bill

What can I say about Bill? He was my surrogate dad. Bill was my science teacher in high school. I had him for physical science, chemistry, and physics. Also, he was one of my football coaches. When I was having trouble in school, be it high school or college, I could always run up to Bill's house for some advice. When I called him to see if he could be a support driver, he just said, "How long do you need me?"

I said at least ten days but probably could use him for a month. He responded, "Whatever you need."

He met me and Nick, who was also a former student of Bill's, in Charleston. We all went out to a very nice, high-end steak house for Easter Sunday. It was ninety-six dollars just for the steak. At this point, I didn't care about the money. It was great having a day off. Hell, I was just so happy to have two of my best friends with me. We drank and ate, and the owner treated us to cordials in honor of my walk. I looked at the menu. They were forty dollars a pop! It was worth every penny. To this day it was the best steak I have ever eaten.

Bill prided himself on giving me the weather report. He did not get the weather report from a TV or radio station. Instead, he went online, looked at cloud formations, and made his own predictions. He was always more accurate than any other weather reports that I looked at.

Also, Bill would always find me a back route, a trail, or a footpath to keep me out of traffic. I always was astounded how he could do this. It made such a difference to me being able to stay off main roads and avoid getting killed! He even talked to some of the managers at our hotels to get my name on the outside billboard. I still remember the first time, driving into the Hampton Inn parking lot with Bill after finishing up on my twenty miles and seeing this huge sign in lights saying, "Hampton Inn Welcomes Richard Albero Wounded Warrior Project"! Little things like that made such a difference.

## Day 65, No Recording.

*Sign entering Hampton Inn.*

Finally, Bill was with me in North Carolina when I hit two real bad days of hard rain. These would be the only two days I would miss on my whole trip. Bill was like a drill sergeant. He really kept me focused. But it had its limits, as we were both type A personalities. So on the second day of rain, he was very conscious of me falling behind schedule. Bill and I were sitting in his car waiting for this torrential rain to stop. It slowed down to "just" a heavy downpour. Bill said to me, "Okay, get out and start walking."

Now we had been together almost a month. Regardless of our strong bond, no doubt, we were starting to get on each other's nerves. So I responded to him in a very loud voice, "You're nuts! I'm not going out in that rain."

Now the two days previous to this, I had walked through high weeds up to my waist (didn't North Carolina folk pay their taxes, and couldn't they mow the weeds on the sides of highways?), waded in swamps, got inundated with bugs, and there were only very, very narrow spots on the side of the road to walk on. The rain kept increasing. Bill said to me again, "Okay, it looks good; get out and get going."

I had reached my max. I retorted, "You're f—kin nuts if you think I'm going to walk out in that rain."

Bill looked at me and knew not to push the envelope.

Another funny thing with Bill was every time he went to get lunch, it got messed up. I kept telling him no cheese or mayo on my hero sandwich. He would tell me he said that when giving the order. After a few days, I was really starting to think Bill was doing it just to bust my chops. Again, with the walking getting to me a little—did I say a little?—my patience was growing shorter. So Bill said he would watch them make the sandwich and guarantee to get it right.

When he came back, he said he'd solved the problem. As he watched them make the sandwich, the kitchen guy started to put the cheese on it. Bill said, "No cheese; I told you that."

The kitchen guy responded, "But it's free."

Bill said, "I don't care; don't put it on."

These guys at the sub shop were so trained to work on an assembly line, they just wouldn't make any changes. Whether you wanted it or not, you got cheese, mustard, and mayo!

Bill finished up his tour in Virginia with me. We hugged outside the hotel, and he said, "Son, you're doing a good job. See you at the stadium." I was so proud that he referred to me as one of his sons. I took it as a real honor. As I said earlier, Bill was the only one besides my children and Joe Girardi who believed I could complete this walk. Without Bill for those thirty days, even with the snoring, I would not have made it. He was my personal drill sergeant!

An excerpt from an interview with Bill while he was my support driver follows:

*I expected it all, and I got it all. All the memories were wonderful. Especially you crawling across the Virginia state line. Keep doing a good job. Keep it up. Don't falter at all. I knew you'd do it from the beginning. I still have that great confidence and faith in your ability to get it done. With or without me, it would have happened. You knew as soon as you took that first step, nothing was going to stop you even if you had to walk in on bloody stumps at the end. Good wishes; keep it up. It's a good spiritual journey, believe me!*

# Chapter 12

# FORTY-NINE HILLS IN VIRGINIA!

Slow motion gets you there faster.
—Hoagy Carmichael

## Day 66—Mileage Walked: 19.14
## (Spotsylvania Courthouse, Virginia)

*I have only eighteen more days. I'm on my way to Fredericksburg. Yesterday I did twenty-five hills; I even amazed myself. Rare that happens, but I really did. I should be in Fredericksburg tomorrow and DC Sunday, with two weeks left. Truly amazing. Going through a whole batch of emotions here. All right, hopefully will stay safe; the weather looks good, and hopefully the hills will chill out a little bit. Ciao!*

## Day 67—Mileage Walked: 18.83 (Stafford, Virginia)

*Hard to believe entering Fredericksburg in another two miles. Actually found sidewalks. Pretty cool! Okay, Carole is now my support driver. I went to bed at seven o'clock last night. I was so beat. I amazed myself, which doesn't happen that often. It's a little bit overcast, which is good. Getting ready for the hoopla in DC. If there is any hoopla. Got a sports interview sometime this afternoon. They're coming down, which is good. Starting to smell the roses. Hard to believe. Just have to suck it up. Seventeen days, soon saying two weeks, which will be really cool. All righty.*

*Just stopped at a food truck in Stafford, Virginia, on Route 1. This guy, probably in his twenties, didn't seem to have a lot of money, came up to me after reading my shirt and asked me if I was hungry, he would buy me lunch. How sweet is that!*

*Just had my interview with the sports channel from DC. What nice people! Diane and David. We stopped at a little restaurant to do the interview. They had a 9/11 memorial on the wall. How coincidental was that? We signed a dollar bill, and they posted it on the ceiling. The owner came up to me and slipped a donation in my hand. Pretty cool.*

***One of the forty-nine hills in Virginia!***

This interview gave me a little boost. How coincidental was it that we stopped at this one place that had a 9/11 memorial? Also, I was fitted with a GoPro camera to my head. This camera allows for hands-free recording. This was really a trip. As I said previously, I tried to get companies with this equipment to sponsor me using their product. A shame they all rejected support except for Tilley and

Sports Water. It would have been nice to have more support. I would have had some wonderful and unique video to share. Diane, the editor from the Washington DC sports channel, was supervising the interview. She made me feel so comfortable. I felt she was doing more than an interview. She was really astonished at what I was trying to accomplish. This made me feel great and proud, not just of myself, but of the Wounded Warrior Project as well.

Many people have marveled at some of my accomplishments on this walk. But the one that sticks out to me the most was walking up forty-nine hills in two days. It was unreal, like I was on autopilot. These hills were not small. I had to play games with myself. I would walk up one big hill. After a few minutes, another one would appear. I just said to myself, "Let's go." It was like Gary was next to me saying, "Just do it, Uncle Rich!" I actually wore out a complete pair of shoes doing all these hills. I contemplated how in the revolutionary times settlers came down these hills with their wagons and horses. They were so steep. I felt so bad for those horses. I wonder how many horses were injured and how many brakes failed on the wagons.

Myself personally, doing all forty-nine hills in two days was one of my most remarkable feats of the trip.

## Day 68—Mileage Walked: 16.12 (Approaching DC)

*Sixteen more days to go. Coming to the two-week mark pretty soon. A lot of crazy stuff going on in DC, I think. On a fairly nice part of Route 1; no hills so far. By some miracle of God, hopefully today will be a good day. Tomorrow will be a long day before checking into DC. Finding the hotel and all that stuff. It is what it is. Getting used to these long days. Everything else seems to be okay. Catching up and keeping up. Tom (my next support driver) wrote a beautiful thing about me on his blog. So hopefully have the strength for today. All righty.*

Here is the article my friend and support driver Tom wrote in his blog ("In the Shade"):

> Rich Albero has a long history as a generous soul. When we taught high school together in New York for twenty-five years, he would occasionally show up to school in the morning looking a bit rumpled and

haggard, perhaps even unshaven. Some would make assumptions based on this appearance. He'd had a rough night, they'd think, or he didn't care about how he looked. Both conclusions were right, but not for the reasons assumed.

I knew that, in fact, Rich had arrived at school having volunteered to help supervise a homeless shelter in his hometown overnight. If he seemed less concerned with his own appearance, it was because he was more concerned with providing a warm meal and a safe bed for others in need. At school, he kept his work at the shelter to himself and asked me not to mention it to anyone. That selfless volunteer spirit spoke to who Rich was.

It came as no surprise to me, then, when Rich began to talk last year about wanting to walk more than twelve hundred miles from Steinbrenner Field in Tampa, Florida, to Yankee Stadium in the Bronx. That grand plan spoke of who he still is.

Rich Albero is sixty-five years old now, retired several years from high school teaching and just this past year from teaching math at Saint Petersburg College, not far from his home in Dunedin, Florida. Having traveled around the world as a young seaman in the United States Merchant Marine, Rich was later to take other trips of note with his nephew Gary Albero—a memorable excursion to the Grand Canyon, for example, or a drive up to Boston to cheer his beloved Yankees as they battled the Red Sox at Fenway.

But now, his grandest of journeys, this trek from Tampa to the Bronx, is a tribute to Gary, who died in the World Trade Center towers on 9/11. True to Rich's and Gary's generous spirits, the walk is raising donations to the Wounded Warrior Project.

The Yankees organization has been very supportive of his walk. In the first week of March, Rich started his journey from home plate at Steinbrenner Field in Tampa, where in the midst of spring training, the Yankees gave him an enthusiastic send-off. "See you in New York," manager Joe Girardi said with a hug.

With some help from a few sponsors—Ionic Sportwater, Brooks shoes, Tilley hats, Wyndham Hotels, and Wish You Were Here Productions, among others—Rich is now well past the halfway point of his journey. Calling on a small cadre of close friends or family as his support drivers, he recently made his way north through the Carolina one step at a time. Now, in early May, with more than eight hundred miles behind him, he has reached the rolling hills of Richmond, Virginia.

As he approaches Washington, DC, I'm to join Rich as his support driver for a week. He'll rise before dawn, do his morning exercises, and then wake me for breakfast. Next, I'll drive him to where he had ended the previous day's walk, and he'll resume his journey, aiming for another twenty miles that day. Around noon, Rich will call to tell me his location. Along with an afternoon's supply of sportwater, I'll bring his lunch and a bucket of ice water to soak his feet midday. Following that, he'll resume his walk until late afternoon or early evening, when I'll pick him up and drive him to our next hotel. After a hearty dinner, it'll be early to bed and up again before dawn.

Rich hopes to reach New York City by Memorial Day weekend. There he will lay a commemorative wreath beneath Gary's name at Ground Zero. He will end his walk with a ceremony at home plate before a game at Yankee Stadium, a fitting conclusion to a selfless journey by a sixty-five-year-old Yankee fan who walked more than twelve hundred miles from spring training

to a home game in the Bronx to honor his nephew and
our wounded warriors.

## Day 69—Mileage Walked: 18.02
## (Fort Belvoir, Virginia)

*Yowzer, yowzer. Tomorrow will end week ten, which means I will be two
weeks from Yankee Stadium. Unbelievable! A little threat of rain today.
God willing, I will make it on time. Carole (my new support driver) is
hanging in there. Lowell, my former student and a softball player, will
walk with her tomorrow. Lowell is mapping out DC for me. I'll go out to
dinner with her and have a day off Tuesday. So I should be able to get
through these next three days. Smelling the roses; can't believe it. [Crying]
It's really becoming a reality. Just have to keep it together. Will see what
DC brings. Hopefully will be able to finally finish up on my soul.*

*Just came up with this great idea. Paint a reflective type of arrow
inside my right arm with a pointer on it. So when I reach out with my
right arm and they see it, they know to move over. Pretty smart.*

*Well, just had an awakening. Was on the phone with Nicky. There
is an underpass with no room on either side. A curve coming into it. I
thought that I could hug it. Had to go on the fast-lane side; the cars came
around, and they were going to hit me. Luckily I just got through enough
to reach a railing, and I literally dove headfirst, laughing now, but I almost went in my pants. Over the railing into the median grass. God was
with me. It was a true, true wake-up call. I can't take chances like that
anymore, I just can't. I just got to realize I am fallible.*

*So, thank God. I'm still shaking.*

This day, day 69, will always be imprinted in my memory banks.
It was almost my last day on earth. I found a shortcut to walk on.
About a quarter mile walking on this shortcut road, I came upon a
one-way tunnel. The tunnel consisted of two lanes, both facing me,
which I thought was a good thing. The room on both sides was negligible. Did I say negligible? Face a wall and put your two hands on the
wall in front of you with elbows bent. That was all the room I had. A
foot, maybe a foot and a half at most. No traffic was coming at all.

My options were either to walk through the tunnel sideways, hugging the sidewall very closely, or retreat back for a quarter mile to the

main highway and exit this tunnel. With all the walking I was doing, retreating backward was not a favorable choice. I was not in favor of adding extra mileage going away from Yankee Stadium! As long as I had room on the side, although extremely narrow, I estimated it was okay to enter the tunnel. What I didn't account for was the blind curve the cars would be traveling on entering the tunnel on the other side. I could not see that curve from my side of the tunnel. When I did see it, it was too late.

As I proceeded walking sideways through the tunnel, hugging the sidewall, I had Nick on the phone. I was telling him about my situation. I was nervous but still confident at that moment. Suddenly as I saw the light at the end of the tunnel, two cars appeared around the curve, traveling about fifty miles per hour. The two cars side by side were driving into the tunnel entrance. I could actually see the expressions on the face of the driver of the car closer to me. Luckily, both drivers of the cars had good reactions, which was "What the hell is this guy doing here?" I could now see the panic on the face of the car driver closer to me. I started literally screaming on the phone to Nick that I was going to die.

He kept yelling back to me, "Rich, Rich."

I kept yelling back to Nick, "I'm going to die." As I came to the end of the tunnel, the car in my lane passed me. At the same moment, I spotted a guardrail at the end of the tunnel as a third car came around the curve. As I exited the tunnel, the third car driver did not see me. I dove over the railing; my legs were still sticking out. I thought for sure the third car was going to hit my legs, cutting them off. As I lay on the grass, shaking, Nick was still yelling in the phone, "Rich, Rich, are you all right?"

I reached down to see if my legs were still connected to my body. I wanted to make sure I wasn't in shock from losing my legs. I looked up to the sky and said, "Thanks, God." I couldn't believe how stupid I was for going into a one-way tunnel with no room on either side. Also, to make matters worse, a curve on the side coming into the tunnel. After this earth-shattering experience, I promised myself I would never be so reckless again. I started to think about my kids having no father and how vulnerable life can be. Maybe this near-death experience was a good thing. From that day on, I made sure not to take any more chances. God had given me a reprieve.

# Day 70—Mileage Walked: 18.50 (Groveton, Virginia)

*Can you believe it? Week 10 is complete! It's a gorgeous day. First time in shirtsleeves, I'm in Arlington, just three miles out of DC. Will be walking through DC on Mother's Day. Today on my way to Baltimore, two weeks to the stadium. I just can't believe it. Truly can't believe it. It's really becoming a reality even after yesterday's close call.*

*When I checked into the Hampton Inn last night, all the people, it was unbelievable. All the employees and top corporate officers came out and shook my hand. When I checked into my room, they had this nice poster hanging on the wall wishing me luck with all these kind sayings. They bought me a foot massager and soap. Just nice people.*

*I didn't get lost getting out of DC this morning, which was great. Meeting Lowell later on. So looking forward to a really good day. I have ESPN tomorrow. So my soul is feeling good today.*

*Officially in DC. Didn't get lost, which is a miracle. Met this Peruvian guy. He said, "You walking?" He couldn't believe I was walking. Here we are, DC.*

*I must have said hello to at least twenty people here in DC. Not one has said hello back. I kept repeating, saying hello. What is the case here? People can't say hello?*

*So I was lost. I met this guy who was so nice. He couldn't speak English very well. He was giving me directions. I then told him that I was not driving.*

*"Okay, take the train then. I will put you on the train."*

*I told him I couldn't go on the train; I was walking.*

*He said, "You don't want to walk. Get on the train."*

*It was pretty comical. I couldn't convince him that I could only walk. He kept shaking his head like I was nuts.*

*I met a nice girl named Michelle. She asked what charity I was walking for. I told her my phone was dead. She took me to a little store that sells these instant chargers. She said she wanted to pay for it, but the store didn't have any. Then she wanted to buy me some water. Told her it was okay. She took a picture of me. What a sweet kid. These acts of kindness keep me going.*

**Interlude 6**

Friends are God's way of taking care of us.

## Carole

How Carole became my support driver was unique. As I started my walk, I kept receiving Facebook messages with religious connotations. I decided to track these messages down. I called my former real estate agent Dawn in Dunedin, who was a good friend of mine. I asked her if she might know who was sending me these emails. She laughed and said yes, that her friend Carole had taken an interest in me. I said okay, it was nice for Carole to send these religious sayings in support.

A short time later as I arrived in Jacksonville, I received a phone call. It was Carole. She apologized for missing the ceremony at Steinbrenner Field kicking off my walk. She got lost coming into Tampa. This was a foreboding. Carole asked to drive up to Jacksonville to meet me. She wanted to bring me a homemade healthy lunch.

I said, "Well, if you want to, but it's a good two-and-a-half-hour car trip."

Carole said she didn't mind. Carole showed up for lunch the next day. She informed me it took her almost seven hours due to navigation issues. I told her how appreciative I was for the visit and the healthy lunch. She reserved a room at the hotel and left early the next morning. My brother was my support driver at the time. I shared with him about Carole's visit. I thought to myself, I probably would not see Carole again. Wrong!

The last week with Bill was coming up. I had no support driver for the interval between when Bill would leave to the time I reached Washington, DC. I was getting nervous about this dilemma. Through Facebook, Carole told me she was attending a presentation in Virginia. On a slim prayer, I called her and asked if she would become my support driver for a week. She said, "Yes." It was so kind of her. I arranged a rental car for her.

God bless Carole's soul. The week being my support driver was probably one of the hardest things she ever did in her life. First, she was so nervous I was going to get run over. Every morning she would say, "Be careful. Don't take any chances." She even purchased a reflective vest for me to wear. I feel bad saying this, but I hated the vest. It made me feel like a lighted beacon and very uncomfortable. However, I made sure to wear it every few days. It was my way of saying thank you to Carole for all her efforts. Finally, after the day of almost getting killed, I started becoming really paranoid. Paranoid about her fears that I was going to get hit by a car or truck on this walk. With all the walking I was doing, fatigue setting in, and my mind starting to go through all kinds of crazy thought processes, a seed of paranoia was planted.

Also, for whatever reason, Carole's week was the worst with traffic conditions. Almost every night returning to our hotel after my day of walking, traffic found us. Carole was my support driver when I was walking up all the hills in Virginia. These hills were killing me. I was really sucking wind. When Carole picked me up, I was usually pretty spent. Then, we would have to drive back to the motel. I remember two nights specifically when it took us over two hours to drive back to the motel. Nothing worse than walking twenty miles of rough terrain and large hills, then having to sit in a car for two hours in bumper-to-bumper traffic.

One night, Route 95 was completely shut down due to a serious car accident. They were diverting all traffic to our road. I had walked about twenty miles that day. So here we were driving back to our hotel and literally crawling along at about ten miles per hour. The ride back to the hotel should have taken about twenty minutes tops! The car in front of us was blasting rap music at the volume of a music concert. I was going nuts. It was on nights like this that I questioned my sanity for doing this walk. After about an hour and a half with stop-and-go traffic, I was ready to jump out of the car and disconnect the radio of the car in front of us. It would have been easy as we were at a standstill in the road.

Carole just wanted to mother hen me to death. She had a heart of gold. I remember one specific time on my lunch break while doing an interview with ESPN. Carole walked right in front of the camera crew and took out a wet rag to wipe my forehead. God bless her soul.

Carole had some issues with a sense of direction. I should have known that from the initial lunch experience. One evening, after getting stuck in traffic, coming back to our hotel after completing my walk for the day, I asked Carole if she would pick up dinner while I showered. I gave her the name of the place, with driving directions. It was only ten minutes down the road. An hour later, I got a call from

Carole informing me she couldn't locate the place! Eventually she found the way back to the hotel.

Without Carole to bail me out, the walk would have stalled. I knew how difficult it was for Carole to navigate her way around unfamiliar territory. Also, how frantic she became each day I went out into the traffic. I think she really believed I was going to get killed. To make matters worse, the traffic conditions on our return home every night to the hotel were really putting me over the edge. At this point in my walk, I was so strung out and void of patience that I don't know how Carole put up with me. She had the patience of a saint.

Later, when I returned to Dunedin, my friend Dawn kept asking if I would appear in front of the town board to be recognized for my walk. I kept refusing. Finally, after a few months, I gave in and agreed with Dawn's request.

The night I appeared at the Dunedin Town Hall, Dawn was with Carole waiting at the front door of the town hall to greet me. We entered together. The mayor and the board of trustees congratulated me. They awarded me a certificate of recognition. When we got outside, I approached Carole to tell her how sorry I was for being so mean when she was my support driver. To Carole's credit, she said that I was not being mean; she realized how worn out each day I was from all the walking—and also the pressure I was under trying to stay alive!

For Carole, as I said, being my support driver was probably the hardest and scariest thing she had done in her life. I will be always grateful for her kindness, perseverance, and prayers.

## Day 71, Week 11—Mileage Walked: 13.69 (Jessup, Maryland)

*Now less than two weeks to New York City. Holy cow! I have to keep my head together and not get too emotional. This time next week in Philly. Will have to wear all my Yankees stuff. Tom comes down today. Carole, God bless her soul, will be going back today. Weather is decent on Route 1.*

*Had such a nice day with Lowell yesterday. She walked about six miles with me. Caught me up on what she is doing. And Hillary and Brianna and my other softball players and ex-students. Went out to dinner. She helped me map out my routes just great, just great. So today hopefully will not be too many hills. Although I see one.*

*When I'm done today, I should be just four miles out of Baltimore. Unbelievable, huh? All right, I will be able to cross this massive highway here. Okay.*

While in DC, Tom became my new support driver. I had an invitation to visit the local Wounded Warrior Project office. On my rest day, Tom and I visited there. While we were given a tour, we passed an open area for new employees. About twenty newbies were waiting for a project manager, who was late to talk to them. They asked me if I would address the crowd. No problem; just like teaching again in front of a classroom.

Luckily I was full of energy with this quasi day off. I told them how fortunate they were to soon be working for the Wounded Warrior Project organization. I shared with them my experience at the Wounded Warrior office in Jacksonville, Florida. How everyone just seemed content and enjoyed their work. I emphasized the point that they had an opportunity to do meaningful work at the DC office and that they should be very proud of their efforts. It must have gone well, as they responded with very nice applause at the conclusion of my brief speech.

While in DC, I kept getting calls from a particular senator. He wanted to meet with me and take a few pictures. Until my TV spot appeared on the DC news, I had never had any contact with this individual. I said okay, but I would only be in DC for one day. It was imperative for me to adhere to my schedule.

The senator's office called me back. They said the senator had fifteen minutes open in his schedule the following evening. They told me I should go to his office for some press pictures at that time.

I told his aide, "Thank you, but I will be in Baltimore by that time and unable to come back to DC."

She was shocked. "You mean you don't want to meet with the senator?"

I responded that was correct.

She repeated the question.

I responded again that it was not possible to meet with the senator. In my mind, this senator's goal was only to get his picture in the papers for some publicity. The icing on the cake was that he did not want to make any effort on his part to make our meeting happen. I just laughed to myself. I had to admit, the aide's reaction was funny. You don't want to meet with the senator? No!

In DC, while doing the interview for the YES channel, I was walking down the steps of the Lincoln Memorial. Two men, who had to be brothers because they looked like twins, were passing me.

The one brother glanced at my shirt and told his brother, "Look, that guy is walking from Tampa to the Bronx."

His brother responded, "No, he isn't. Probably wearing the shirt to look cool and palm some money."

I just started laughing and continued down the stairs.

The interview with the YES TV crew was in the proximity of the Vietnam Memorial. The one thing I remember most about this interview was tearing up and making this statement: "I want everybody who lost somebody on 9/11 to think of some quality of that person and share it with ten, twenty people, and maybe that will make it all worth it." That was my mantra. This was my walk in its pure essence.

All the news clippings, radio interviews, and celebrity status didn't mean much to me. I didn't understand at the time why I was crying so much, but it was my body's way of telling me what was really important. Really remember those poor souls who lost their lives on 9/11. The amount of goodness they had in their hearts to share. It was up to us to take up the burden of their goodness. For every individual of 9/11 who unfortunately lost their opportunity to do some kindness in this world, we needed to take that burden. We needed to realize it was our moral obligation to disseminate the kindness lost by 9/11 victims. That was what my walk was about. My soul was reaching out to me with each of my tears. More and more I was starting to understand what my walk was truly about.

## Day 72—Rest Day, Mileage Walked: 0

## Day 73—Mileage Walked: 13.77 (Elkridge, Maryland)

*Outside of Baltimore. Don (soundman from the ESPN TV crew) came back. He brought Tom (my new support driver) and me lunch. What a great guy. On Route 7 now. Have sidewalks, which is not bad; not a lot of traffic. Really doing well so far. First day doing twenty miles.*

*Stopped at a bar, met Dineca the owner, and went to the bathroom. She wanted to know what I was doing. Wanted to take her picture with me. A couple of people said they heard about me on the radio. So it was really neat. They saw me when I stopped for lunch. Daniel, the ESPN guy, is still with me. Tom is trying to find us. Hopefully everything will be okay. Learning about dogs that growl with a southern accent. They're not the friendliest in the world.*

Don was a sound person who was working with the ESPN crew in DC doing my interview at the Hampton Inn. He was very impressed with my interview. Don offered to meet me in Baltimore and walk with me. He shared with me that he grew up in Baltimore. Don said he knew all the shortcuts throughout the city. I said, "Great."

Don met me as I started my walk in Baltimore. He had only one small bottle of water with him and was wearing sandals! Don also had a little bit of a beer belly which was okay because he had such a big heart. I said, "Don, are you sure you want to do this?" I was definitely hesitant when seeing his walking shoes were sandals.

He said, "No problem." He started to walk with me. It was really a hot day out. I was convinced after a quarter mile he would give up. Wrong! For the next eight miles or so, Don gave me a once-in-a-lifetime historical perspective of Baltimore. He guided me through the back streets of Baltimore. It was like having my own historical personal guide.

His knowledge of Baltimore was unbelievable. We stopped for lunch at a famous establishment. Unfortunately, I have forgotten its name. While there, some of the customers recognized me from viewing TV clips of my walk. They asked if they could take some pictures with me. I still didn't understand the fascination about taking pictures with me. I was just a guy walking to the Bronx. I was so tired by lunchtime, I just wanted to rest, not deal with all this hoopla.

Don said he was done for the day. I said, "Give me your phone number, address, and your last name so I can post it on Facebook. Also, if I ever write a book, I want to be sure to mention you in it."

He just laughed and said, "That's okay; just remember me as Don."

I will never forget that tour with him walking in sandals with such little water, a truly giving person who did this out of his respect for me. It doesn't get any better than that. Don's kindness gave me quite a boost for the next couple of days when things got tougher. His kindness to me will never be forgotten.

ESPN had assigned a professional photographer named Daniel to walk with me through Baltimore. Daniel was a long-distance runner. He had no trouble at all keeping up with me that day in Baltimore. This included walking backward and running ahead of me or running across the street to take pictures. We had many great conversations together. He promised to release any pictures he could to me after his commitment with ESPN ended. Daniel took over six hundred shots that day. Eventually, only five shots would be chosen for the article soon to appear in the ESPN magazine. True to his word, Daniel sent me the other pictures.

It was good people like Don and Daniel who helped me overlook some of the nonsupportive people during my walk. Also, while Daniel was with me, my shoes were starting to hurt my feet. I needed to get a replacement pair. Daniel knew of a huge wholesale sneaker warehouse not too far away from the hotel where I was staying. After completing my mileage for the day, Tom, Daniel, and I went to get my replacement sneakers. The place was huge. It had a great assortment of walking shoes. I explained to the manager about my walk, and Daniel showed him his credentials from ESPN. I asked if he could give me some kind of discount on the shoes (actually hoping he would donate them). I offered to advertise his place on my website. He said the price was the price! Throughout my walk, I never could understand this philosophy.

## Day 74—Mileage Walked: 16.99 (Rossville, Maryland)

*By myself again. Makes me feel a little bit lonely. My second day walking toward Philly, which means I have four or five days before I get there. Then New York, New York. Saw the clip on DC. Diane did such a great job. Hopefully this Route 7 is going to be nice to me today. Can't get over Don and Daniel getting me through the bad sections of Baltimore. Tom is doing a good job. Doing some traveling. Had to buy two more pairs of shoes because my feet were hurting so bad. From the beginning, they seem to be pretty good. Hopefully they will hold up, and I won't have to walk with pain anymore. Little chilly today; hopefully it will warm up and be just right. Another twenty-mile day coming. Hopefully I can work in a day's rest before getting to New Jersey.*

## Day 75—Mileage Walked: 14.05 (Aberdeen, Maryland)

*Screaming out loud at the top of my lungs. I just hit a thousand miles— hey, everybody, a thousand miles on day 75 about sixty-eight miles outside of Philly. It's unbelievable!* [Crying] *I just can't believe it; I'm doing it, still looking for my soul. But I'm doing it. Lord, thank you, thank you. Well, Gary I hope you're looking down. Mom, Dad, Andy, Grandma, keep me safe. I still have a ways to go. I hope ... I don't know what I hope. I do hope this helps somebody become a better person.*

When walking through a street in Wilmington, Delaware, Tom spotted a police car parked on the side of the road and approached it. He informed the officer about my walk.

As I came up to the car, the officer said, "Hold on for a minute." When he disconnected from his radio, the police officer shared with me about an incident a week before. An individual doing a run for cancer was mugged. He was still in the hospital with his injuries! The police officer received permission to be my personal escort through the streets of Wilmington. The police chief did not want a repeat of the previous week's mugging incident. That worked for me!

This was great. The police car stayed a few yards ahead of me as I walked. People outside sitting and socializing on their stoops just looked at me, trying to figure out what was going on. While walking, a big hill—and I mean a huge hill—appeared in front of me.

The police officer stopped his car. I walked up to the car. He suggested, "C'mon. I will give you a ride to the top." Insinuating nobody would know.

I responded, "Although tempting, I can't. It wouldn't be right; I have to walk it."

He looked at me with respect in his eyes and said, "Okay, your choice."

I was proud of my integrity, even when I would have loved to have jumped into that police car for a ride to the top of the hill. I was very appreciative of the police escort. It reduced a great amount of tension as I walked through the city.

*Entering Delaware.*

## Day 76—Mileage Walked: 20.01 (Elkton, Maryland)

*I'm about forty miles out of Philly. Hard to believe. Had breakfast at Elton diner where the waitress was really hot stuff. Let us take a couple of pictures with Marilyn Monroe pictures all over the place. It was a good way to start the day. She was a lot of laughs. After we took the pictures, she said she didn't want to see any of them on Facebook with her clothes off.*

*So, eight more days. Can you believe that? Eight more days. This time next week, I will be knocking on New York City's door. My body is really starting to be sore. I'll try to get a massage in Philly. See what I can do. Change reservations, so we stay in Philly.*

*Tom's just been superlative. It's one of the other great things about this trip. All my best friends I got to spend some quality time with. I don't know if they look at it the same way.*

*Again, a couple of cars tried to run me over. Look left and want to come out quick. It is what it is. Hopefully the rain will stay off. I will get my twenty miles in today. These hills are killing me, though. My legs are sore for the first time. I have a cold. Everything is part of the beast.*

*Couple of more days should be in New Jersey. That will be unbelievable.*

*Yesterday hit the one-thousand-mile-mark, as you know. Really went crazy. So looking for a good day, overcast right now, plenty of space to walk, have sidewalks. Really hope to take advantage of it.*

Surprisingly, the most dangerous areas for getting hit by a car were the strip malls. Numerous times, I'd be walking on the sidewalk approaching a mall exit where a driver would be looking to his or her left for a slight break in traffic. Their intent was to hit the gas and shoot out to the right as soon as they saw an opening in the traffic on the left. Guess who was on the right! Several times it was the same scenario. Sometimes they couldn't dart out on the road immediately. As I walked in front of the car, I would knock on their hood with my hand so they knew I was there. After almost getting hit several times, I would become very frustrated. So when approaching a car waiting to dart out, I would yell, "Hey!" They would look to their right upon suddenly hearing my voice. Their reaction was priceless. On the plus side, when I returned home, I became such a better driver, especially when exiting from strip malls!

**Interlude 7**

Friends are the siblings God never gave us.
—Mencius

**Tom**

I had known Tom since 1984. We both taught at the same high school in Westchester County. He was the chairperson of the English department. I was a mathematics instructor. At that time, all the math instructors' offices were in one wing. In a different wing, the English instructors' offices were housed. We both decided to break with tradition and shared an office together. My vocabulary really increased over the years sharing that office with Tom. In return, Tom's craziness increased thanks to me. Even as a math teacher, I cannot add up how many good laughs and times we shared.

One time we were doing a pub crawl in New York City. We were sitting in the corner of McSorley's famous alehouse having a few beers. A short time later, through the front door, a tour guide entered with a group of young female teachers. We recognized two of our colleagues. Well, they were shocked at seeing formal Tom drinking beer in the corner with me. I asked what they were doing. They informed us they were taking a summer class on the history of New York for a credit-pay increase. Part of the course was making a historical stop at McSorley's for a beer.

Tom retorted, "Hell, if I knew I could get credit for drinking beer, I would have enrolled in that class a long time ago."

Tom was so honest and righteous in such a good way. He was buying a bedroom furniture set for his two boys. The salesman was giving him a great price but was being rude and borderline dishonest with the deal. Tom said he would get back to him. Tom found a more reputable salesperson at another store. Out of courtesy, he went back to the original store to inform the salesperson he was buying the furniture from another store. The salesperson could not believe it. He kept repeating his price was cheaper. As Tom said to me the next day in our office, "He just didn't get it." Integrity was worth so much more!

An excerpt from an interview with Tom while being my support driver follows:

*Well, I didn't expect Rich to see how dangerous the roads he was walking along were. Even with the wide areas on Route 140 and 13, there's not the room you think. There are people turning off the road and not room for you when you think there is. I didn't expect to see how fatigued he was. Of course he wouldn't admit it. After fourteen miles in the morning and another six in the evening, he was pretty much out of it for a while. I'd give him time and room to decompress and come back to us! It's been an experience for me. I was very glad to do this for Rich and give him that support. It just added to my admiration of what he was doing.*

## Day 77—Mileage Walked: 18.58
## (Marcus Hook, Pennsylvania)

*Week 11's over, only one week to go. Let me repeat that … one week to go!*

*Well, I got a bad cold and went to bed at six thirty last night. Hopefully will be able to fight through it.*

*Still bearing down on Philly. Will be staying in a Philly hotel tonight. Which is great. Hopefully the rain won't come. We stopped at the Bear*

*Diner this morning. The waitress was so sweet. She gave us a couple of dollars of her tip money for the walk. Kind people out there. We met some troopers. They looked so young to be carrying guns.*

*One of them said to me, "Are you a northerner boy?" We were asking for directions through Philly. They were telling us about the hood and warning us to be careful. Tom's last day; Scott comes tonight. Sure Scott will be able to handle the two days pretty readily. Could be in New Jersey tomorrow. It all depends. Hope today works out all right.*

As I entered Philadelphia, Scott became my support driver for the next two days. Scott was a colleague of mine for over twenty-three years while working in Westchester County. Scott drove through Philly scouting the roads ahead of me. He became very worried. Scott would say. "Rich, you're nuts. Skip this area; you're going to get mugged or knifed!"

I would laugh. At this point, I foolishly felt invincible. As I walked through some parts of South Philly, there were gangs literally on every end of each street and hookers on the other end. I don't even know how to describe the wheeling and dealing that was going on in the middle of the streets. My head was again like an owl, swiveling constantly, on alert for trouble. As I walked through South Philly, people gawked at me. I had this Rocky look—who is this guy? they wondered!

At one point while I was walking, I suddenly became conscious of something in front of me. I realized it was Scott in front of me waving his hands like crazy.

"Rich, Rich, I have been honking my horn at you forever. I just parked the car, jumped out, ran over here. I have been waving my hands in front of you for a while now."

I responded, "Sorry, I just get so focused."

He was begging me to skip the next area coming up. He told me that I wouldn't come out alive. Na, I was Richard, King of the Walkers, and I had Saint Christopher and Saint Francis on either side of me. I'd never seen Scott so concerned. Scott's grave concern for me showed what a good friend he really was.

This incident in Philly reminded me of particular times with my brother Mikey. When he picked me up at lunchtime, he would always say, "Hey, did you see that lake or that house or whatever?"

I would say, "No."

He looked at me like I was nuts! "How could you not see that big lake?"

What Mikey didn't understand was how focused I had to be on walking and watching literally every car that approached me. I hadn't noticed anything else. I had to be alert in case cars or trucks just veered a few inches to the right. Otherwise, I'd be roadkill. This constant concentration on cars and trucks approaching me was many times more taxing than the physicality of the walk.

## Day 78, Week 12—Mileage Walked: 9.71 (Lansdowne, Pennsylvania)

*Well, I already walked a mile in New Jersey and still have tears coming down my eyes. Just can't believe it, can't believe it. So excited. So excited.*

## Day 79—Mileage Walked in the Morning: 12.27 (Trenton, New Jersey)

*I'm in New Jersey, I'm in New Jersey, I'm in New Jersey, I'm in New Jersey, I'm in New Jersey. I can't believe it. I'm on Route 206, Broad Street, Trenton, heading north. I should be in Princeton today. I cannot believe it; I cannot believe it!*

## Day 80—Mileage Walked: 20.22 (New Brunswick, New Jersey)

*In New Brunswick heading up to Woodbridge. Should hit Woodbridge tomorrow. Friday should hit Newark, Saturday Fort Lee, and then I'm done except for the bridge. Day 80 hopefully will be able to stay on this nice 27 and have sidewalks for quite a while. Got a blister on my foot again. It is what it is. Running out of time to have one day pain free. All right, stay with me.*

**Interlude 8**

Things are never quite as scary when you've got a best friend.
—Bill Watterson

Scott

I have known Scott since 1986, when we formed a special, weird kind of bond. We both had this hidden Walter Mitty personality. It was crazy. The two of us could exchange our thoughts and immediately understand how nuts they were. I could elaborate, but that would be trouble!

Unfortunately, my tape of Scott's interview was damaged. Having Scott there for those two days before entering my home state of New Jersey was just what the doctor ordered. I'll always cherish the memory of seeing Scott actually worried about me and genuinely caring for my well-being.

## Day 82—Mileage Walked: 17.17 (Newark, New Jersey)

*Just about entering the city of Newark. Looking at the sign right now. Coming up to the fourteen-mile mark. I could end it tomorrow and be in Fort Lee. Still cold here. At least have sidewalks. Route 26 was a godsend thanks to Nick. Mixed emotions for sure. A lot to think about what's coming.*

## Day 83—No Audio, Mileage Walked: 19.22 (Bogota, New Jersey)

## Day 84—Mileage Not Recorded (North Arlington, New Jersey)

*It's Friday. I'm sitting under an American flag in front of a deli eating a double egg with ham on a hard roll. Doesn't get much better than that. Sitting almost directly across from Queen of Peace High School, who I played against when I was in high school. I had a ninety-five-yard touchdown callback. Gee, I sound like a High School Harry! Amazing.*

*It felt weird leaving Hampton Inns, knowing it was the last time I would be staying and sleeping there and having breakfast. With a little luck will hit the George Washington Bridge today. Then have two days off! I will be in Westwood, my hometown. I will be walking through*

*Hackensack, where I was born. So a lot of nostalgia, a lot of nostalgia. The weather is good.*

*One of the things I came up with while walking was that the Wounded Warrior Project has this expression: "Thank you for your service." For a lot of military, it's their catchphrase. I'm coming up with this new phrase now that I'm working on it. Something like when I meet a wounded warrior, I'm not going to say, "Thank you for your service." I'm going to say something along the line of "I'm going to do something good in honor of your service." To me it has more meaning. Maybe I will get them to change it over. Because again, people, that makes you think. It makes you responsible to really remember these guys ... It doesn't hurt to be real, to be yourself.*

One thing I sorely missed living in Florida was a double egg with ham on a hard roll. Every time I visited friends and family in New York or New Jersey, the very next morning it was a trip to the local deli for that egg sandwich. When I was going through the last leg of this walk through New Jersey, I could smell the ham in the local Polish delis.

During this time, Jimmy, my support driver, came to check on me. I was sitting on a stool outside one of those Polish delis eating my double egg with ham sandwich. Jim knew my history about these egg sandwiches. He asked me how many I had. I sheepishly admitted to him it was my third deli that I had stopped at that morning to eat an egg sandwich. He just laughed.

As I passed Hackensack Hospital, it was difficult to recognize it. The hospital had gone through many new renovations. At the moment I was walking by it, I realized it had been sixty-five years since I was born in that hospital.

I was born at 12:43 a.m. For several years while my parents were alive, I would call them on my birthday at exactly 12:43 a.m. My mother would always answer the phone. I would have a shot of whiskey at my side. I would toast my mother for bringing me into this world. She would then tell me the annual story about how hard it was raining the night I was born. How my dad almost missed the exit on Route 4 driving to the hospital. We would laugh together, both of us realizing during the conversation how much we loved each other. Now on the flip side, my mother would wake my father, who would get on the phone. His first remark would be, "Do you know what time it is?" He would eventually loosen up. I would thank him for being my father. It was a nice tradition. Unfortunately, now that both are deceased, it has ended. But still, on most of my birthdays, I get up at 12:43 a.m., pour myself a shot, and toast my parents!

As I approached the George Washington Bridge from Fort Lee, I hit one last monster hill. Jimmy, who was scouting the route ahead, warned me about the size of this hill. Once the hill was in sight, it still caught me by surprise. I really believed I was through with all the big hills. In a way, I was right. This hill wasn't big—it was gigantic, almost a mountain. It was the end of the day. I truly had to summon up everything I had to go up that humongous hill. Truly, in every sense, I was now running on empty. This hill was part of the Palisades cliffs geography. This was formerly the location of a famous amusement park.

# Day 85, Week 13—Mileage Walked: 2.46 (Fort Lee, New Jersey)

*Monday, believe it or not, I am walking across the George Washington Bridge. Now looking at the skyline of New York. Not looking over the bridge, of course. I'm on the final six-mile leg where I will see Yankee Stadium, but I won't be walking into it until tomorrow night. The toll is now, I believe, twelve dollars. When I was a kid, it was fifty cents. How things have changed! Thinking about this all the time going through the Carolina. Now actually being here is unbelievable. Hopefully will be across this GW Bridge and will have some comments as I walk down to Yankee Stadium.*

One of the local New York TV cameramen was waiting for us on the Fort Lee side of the bridge. His intent was to walk across the bridge interviewing me. As we started to walk across the bridge, several police cars came up beside us and waved us over. After a brief conversation, we were informed that no TV crews were allowed to film on the bridge without a prior permit. With no permit, the cameraman said he would meet us on the other side. However, before reaching the other side of the bridge, the cameraman called me. He informed me he had been reassigned to another shoot and wished me luck! At this point, nothing was a big deal to me. I just wanted to finish!

As I was walking across, who beeped his horn? Believe it or not, but it was David from Myrtle Beach! I could not believe it was David.

After reaching the other side of the George Washington Bridge, my entourage now consisted of Nick, my son, Dante, and my daughter, Felicia. We started the final hurrah walking down the street to the stadium. No cameras, no crowds, just Gary and my family looking down from above with a lot of pride on their faces.

As far as my reaction, it was nothing earth-shattering. This was just the final lap. I was happy but not crazy over the top. We didn't stop for any drinks, as I was still too focused on arriving at the stadium. Having my son, Dante, daughter, Felicia, and best friend Nick with me, who needed anything more?

As I walked across Macombs Bridge approaching Yankee Stadium in all its glory, I stopped and stared at this magnificent historical building. No goose bumps or any other atypical reaction. I felt a serene calming experience throughout my body. I had completed my walk. I knew since stepping on home plate in Tampa, Florida, I would make it. Sure, I was sixty-five years old and in average shape, but I was one determined son of a gun!

Maybe I didn't go crazy because the other more important aspects of the walk were not evident to me at this moment. Did I make people more aware of wounded warrior issues? Did I find my soul? Did the walk inspire people to share kindness in themselves with others?

The trip was near completion. All I had to do was walk into the stadium tomorrow night and step on home plate. The end! Finito! I was done! Over! Complete! I was still in limbo; it was not sinking in. Everybody was going crazy about my walk. I really didn't care about the publicity. I just wanted to do some good. I wanted my heart to feel good! I wanted my heart to recognize whose body it was in.

*Walking across George Washington Bridge.*

That weekend I made contact with David. I asked if I could visit him at the clothing store he managed. The store was only a short distance from my hotel. My hotel room in New York City was compliments of the New York Yankees. When I met David, I asked him if he had any contacts for a discount on a tuxedo rental. I needed a tuxedo to attend the yearly fund-raising event for the Wounded Warrior Project at the Waldorf Astoria, which was the next night after the Yankee game. David said he would check it out for me and see what he could do.

That weekend, before throwing out the first pitch at Yankee Stadium, I was staying at Nick's apartment in Westwood, New Jersey. David called me there. He told me he was going to drive over from his house. He wanted to take some measurements of me. When he arrived at Nick's place, he informed me that he had a clothing supplier

125

willing to donate a brand-new tuxedo to me in honor of doing my walk. I couldn't believe it! David took my measurements. He said the tux would be ready Wednesday. I could come for a fitting at his store, which I did.

The tux fit like a glove. I had a pair of red and black sneakers on. David saw them. He said I should wear them with my tux to the Wounded Warrior Project Gala. I thought he was nuts. He said people would go crazy over them. At this point, after almost twelve hundred miles of walking, I was game for anything.

When it was time to go to the gala, I was early. I took a seat on the lobby couch with my legs crossed. While waiting, six different ladies made comments on how cool my sneakers were. Of course, I just took it all in!

As a side note, every time I have worn that tuxedo since, I have made a point of wearing those sneakers. At every event, they were a hit.

I returned to Dave's store before going home to Florida. I had purchased some special cigars for him (David was an avid cigar smoker) to show how grateful I was. He was so appreciative. His acts of kindness to me will always be remembered. Again, it was those kind acts that gave me the strength to complete my walk.

On the topic of acts of kindness, while staying at Nick's house, I needed the T-shirt I wore during my walk cleaned and ironed. The Yankees PR department wanted me to wear the same shirt I had worn at the beginning of my walk at Steinbrenner Field in Tampa. I stopped at Emerson Dry Cleaners in New Jersey. He cleaned and ironed my shirt for free. How sweet!

Still in Westwood, I went to an Italian market on Saturday morning for—what else?—a double egg with ham on a hard roll! The man waiting on us listened to Nick talk about the details of my walk. He wanted to share this information with his father, who was in the back of the shop doing prep work. As he started to walk to the back of the shop, his father came out. Seeing me, he smiled and said he was listening to the sports radio channel. The sports announcer had just mentioned about my walk. We all laughed together. Breakfast was free. Pretty cool!

Finally, while visiting my hometown in Washington Township, Jimmy had arranged for me to have a foot massage on his tab. I cannot put into words or anything for that matter how good that foot massage felt. I wanted to hug, kiss, shout out loud to the nice young masseuse but knew I'd probably get arrested. I thought that I was truly in heaven. God bless Jimmy!

Monday morning I did an appearance on the WPIX TV morning show. It still felt strange getting makeup put on. At least I didn't have a nightmare about the morning show producer! The hosts of the show were very gracious. I answered some questions about the walk, and then I was out of there.

May 26 had arrived. The final day of my walk; Yankee Stadium, here I come! First thing was my breakfast, yes, double eggs with ham on a hard roll! I was pretty chill even though that night I was throwing out the first pitch at Yankee Stadium. I would be walking in from the outfield accompanied by some wounded warriors. My son, Dante, had joined me at the hotel. My daughter, Felicia was coming a little later. I was mostly on cloud nine, literally putting one foot ahead of the other.

I took a cab to Stan's. After several games, Gary and I had stopped here to have a Guinness. I walked in. The pregame crowd had started arriving. Now all my children were in attendance. Many friends and other people were coming up to congratulate me. As time went on, Mike, the manager of Stan's, allowed me to stand up on top of the bar and yell to the crowd, "Hey, I just walked from Tampa, Florida, to the Bronx, New York, to honor my nephew Gary!"

The crowd was saying, "Who is this nut on the bar?" But soon it became quiet.

I yelled, "Here's to Gary!"

They all started shouting and screaming. At this moment I was in a different stratosphere.

Looking back, considering all my walking experiences, the kind people I met, stepping on home plates both at Steinbrenner Field and Yankees Stadium, the truly greatest moment was standing on Stan's bar, giving that toast to Gary. In my head, I was thinking, "Gary, who would believe it? I made it!"

*Toasting Gary at Stan's.*

Well, it was time to move out and proceed to the stadium. I had to meet news reporters and TV crews outside the stadium at the Big Bat outside. It was overwhelming. There had to be at least ten TV, radio, and news reporters. One reporter wanted me to take my shoes and socks off to film my feet. I was actually going to do it until my kids starting yelling at me, "Dad, don't do that. It's gross."

Reporters were shooting questions at me left and right. Ed Randle was standing nearby, and that was comforting. Ed approached me and gave me a kiss on the cheek. He said, "Congratulations." He told me he wanted to take me and my family out to dinner the next time I was up in New York City.

*My children.*

The interviews finally ended. A group of wounded warriors joined me as I walked into the stadium. One of the wounded warriors noticed the sunglass marks on each side of my head. He told his companions, "Look at the marks; he is one of us." He told me they all had the same marks from wearing sunglasses in Iraq. I felt very humble at that moment. I felt a kindred spirit within my soul.

As we approached the stadium, people were just cheering and cheering for me. I was saying to myself, "Yes, this is pretty cool." We walked around to the back of the stadium. We had to go through a security gate that had spikes that came up from the ground. This reminded me of the security when I visited West Point. At the gate entrance was Jennifer Steinbrenner Swindal, daughter of George Steinbrenner, Jason Zillo, and Deborah Tymon (senior vice president of marketing). Deborah Tymon was very instrumental working with Andrew Levy in getting me to the stadium, throwing out the first pitch, and God knows how many other things. She was very thorough and gracious. I am truly indebted to her for her professionalism and kindness.

I remember saying to myself how impeccably Jennifer Steinbrenner

Swindal was dressed. She just exuded class! After the introductions, she kissed me on the cheek and whispered in my ear, "Don't tell anybody, but I'm really cheering for the Tampa Bay Lightning, not the Rangers." The Rangers and Tampa were playing against each other in the NHL playoffs. I just smiled at her, thinking how down-to-earth she was.

We proceeded to a gate and entered a tunnel. I was flabbergasted at the size and scope of the stadium's back side. I could see the field as we entered through the security gate. I walked up to the opening. I stared at the famous Yankee Stadium façade above home plate. I could visualize my nephew Gary sitting on the façade with a huge smirk on his face, with my parents and grandparents beside him. I high-fisted them. Then I heard a loud noise to the left of me. It was coming from the suite the Yankees had donated for my use. More than seventy of my friends attended the game. They were screaming at the top of their lungs when they saw me in the tunnel.

Finally the moment had come. The wounded warriors gathered around me, forming a circle. We all clasped hands in the middle. We chanted "Wounded Warriors" and raised our hands to the sky. I started to walk around to the edge of left field. It was nuts. Over the loudspeaker came the voice of Paul Olden announcing, "Please give your attention to the left field area and give a warm welcome to Richard Albero, who will be walking in to touch home plate. He has just completed a walk of twelve hundred miles from Steinbrenner Field in Tampa, Florida, to home plate here at Yankee Stadium. He has raised over thirty-one thousand dollars for the Wounded Warrior Project."

As I walked down the left field foul line just watching all the people standing and clapping, I kept saying to myself, "Who are they cheering for?" It was like an out-of-body experience. "Who is this person walking down the third base line? Who is he?"

*Wounded warriors and I walking down the left field line.*

*The final step.*

Joe Girardi had all the Yankee players standing at the first base line to greet me. As I came up to home plate, I stopped, raised my foot, took a deep breath, and said to myself, "Thank you, God." I then stepped on home plate.

As I walked up to the Yankee players standing on the first base line, the first person I grabbed and hugged was Joe Girardi. I told him, "Thanks for believing in me." I then proceeded to shake the hand of every Yankee standing on the first base line.

Immediately after the last handshake, the Yankees cleared the field. Jennifer Swindal came out and presented me with a check for $25,000 donated by the New York Yankees for the Wounded Warrior Project.

I was overwhelmed. A Yankee official came up to me and asked me to throw out the first ball. Another gentleman handed me a baseball. I looked at the ball and remember saying to myself, "Hell, they're not even giving me a new ball," as it looked used. But suddenly I remembered all the new balls are rubbed with mud so they look worn. I just laughed to myself. They asked if I wanted to stand out in front of home plate and throw it. I said, "Hell, no! I want to throw it from the mound."

*Twenty-five-thousand-dollar donation by*
*The New York Yankees Foundation.*

I walked out to the mound. Adam Warren was the starting pitcher for the Yankees. He wished me luck and smiled. I wanted to tell him that during my walk, I did an interview at his high school. I had asked one of the coaches after that interview if the school had any famous baseball grads. She said only one: "Adam Warren!" I wanted to tell him that but didn't want to distract from his concentration pitching the start of the game.

I was on the mound. Crazy, but I felt the hand of God with me. I took a full windup and threw a perfect, and I mean perfect, strike to home plate. I just knew I was going to throw a strike. The catcher, John Ryan Murphy, came out and handed me the ball. I fist-bumped him on the chest. I told him that I had been following him since A-ball in Florida. Every year since moving to Florida, I would go to several spring training games and pick out a Yankee farmhand I thought would make it to the majors. John Ryan Murphy was my pick a few years back. I had been following his career since. So how coincidental was it that these two Yankees would make up the pitching battery that night?

*Throwing out the first pitch—a strike.*

When I threw out the pitch, I could hear my son near the Yankees dugout yelling, "Holy cow, he threw a strike!" Later, he came up to

133

me to show a text from one of his friends who googled him that only 3 percent of the people who throw out a first pitch from the mound reach home plate, let alone throw a strike. I just laughed. I always could throw strikes when I pitched as a kid. My son, Dante, was just beaming.

It was nice to note that Andrew Levy and Robert Michaels were on the field as well. It was a complete 360!

So the big moment was over. I was led through the dugout into the Yankee batting cages area, where A-Rod was taking batting practice off a pitching machine. He stopped, gave us a glance, and then started hitting again. We then proceeded into a press area. When I sat behind this table, it suddenly hit me that this was the same area where Joe Girardi gave his postgame interviews. I said to myself, "Pretty cool."

After the interview, I went to visit Andrew Levy's private suite and greet his guests. Mickey Rivers was there. I went up to him and asked if he remembered me from the party in Tampa. He said, "Sure. My feet hurt like yours do now." Mickey Rivers was noted in his playing days to walk as if he had sore feet. Yet he was one of the fastest players of his time. I just laughed and asked if he would come join me in my guest suite to meet my family and friends. He said, "No problem."

We walked out of Andrew's suite and proceeded to walk down the corridor to my guest suite. As we passed several other suites with female attendants standing outside the entrance doors, Mickey greeted them all by name. Each one of them would come running up to Mickey and give him a kiss. He just smiled at me as we continued to walk together. As we entered my guest suite, I had my arm around Mickey's shoulder.

My son was the first to see us and said, "Holy crap, that's Mickey Rivers!"

Everybody started clapping for us. Later, my son told me that my daughter Felicia, who was outside the suite in the game seating area, was looking through the glass. She came in and asked Dante, "Who's the old guy with the gold tooth with Dad?"

The suite was great. We had plenty of food and drinks for everybody. I tried to get around to everybody and say hello. Gary's son Michael and his mother were in attendance as well.

One of the wounded warriors came up to me. He said, "Relax. If you need anything, come to one of us. We are your brothers now.

Need a hot dog, a beer, or whatever, just come to us. We have your back." I truly cannot put into words the feeling I had at that moment. I was truly blessed!

Time was going by at warp speed. People were being introduced to me, along with others whom I had not seen in so many years. Three of my colleagues from the high school I taught with in Westchester County were there. One of them came up to me and slipped $200 in my pocket. She whispered in my ear that she knew what a financial burden the trip was on me. I was so grateful for her act of kindness.

Coincidentally, in a few days, I received good news from the Wounded Warrior Project. They had solicited a contributor to cover all my expenses on the walk. When I first submitted my expense account, they called and said my voucher had to be more than that. I said yes it was because I had submitted only major costs. They instructed me to resubmit the voucher with all validated expenses. I did. I was very grateful to the Wounded Warrior Project for covering these costs.

After the game, several of us proceeded back to Stan's. After a few more hours of celebrating, the night finally came to an end. I said my goodbyes and took a taxi back to my hotel. I was feeling no pain. I felt suspended in time. All the hype, cheering, and accolades were nice, but I just remember thinking all I wanted to do was some good. My hope was it would rub off on other people to do the same.

*Chapter 13*

# GARY

Life is short!
Make haste to be kind.
—Henri Amiel

The morning after the game, I met Gary's wife, his son, Michael, his brother, Andy, Dante, and the president of the 9/11 Memorial Museum at Ground Zero. We walked over to Gary's memorial plaque. I placed a Yankee hat and a rose on the plaque. I noticed Andy, Gary's brother, was standing a little hesitantly behind me. Later, I understood why. It was Andy's first visit here to see Gary's memorial since 9/11.

Placing my hand and dripping my tears on Gary's plaque brought a fitting closure to my walk. I believe Gary will always be here with me. I ask him in my prayers every day to watch over my son, Dante, and keep him safe. Not to be redundant, but hopefully my walk will give a chance for people to take some goodness that existed in the people who perished in 9/11 and share it with friends, relatives, and even enemies.

## Chapter 14

# DID I FIND MY SOUL?

*"Kindness Costs Nothing"*—A poster with this inscription was given to me approximately thirty years ago by a former student to post in my classroom. It now hangs in my office at home.

**Poster made by a former student.**

I never actually sat down and weighed the positives or negatives of my walk. To me, it was a very personal experience with my own soul. To reaffirm my strengths, my weaknesses, and the need to give and receive love.

When I started this adventure, I did not have any specific goals. I was not seeking glory or to be a movie star! In retrospect, obviously the first goal was to complete the walk. I never thought about not completing it. People always asked me if I ever thought about quitting.

Call it confidence, conceit, or whatever, but I had no doubt this first goal was going to be accomplished. The second goal was to raise money for the Wounded Warrior Project. To honor those who had served our country. It was great; the final count was approximately $56,000.

Other goals I never really verbalized, but they were in my heart. I really wanted to show the world was a good place. I wanted to re-affirm to myself what loving was about. Sharing the hardships with other people during the walk, giving actual evidence that kindness costs nothing. So many people gave me a hug, shook my hand, or shared a story, reinforcing that kindness costs nothing. These small acts of kindness fortified my soul. They gave me the strength to put one foot ahead of the other.

Walking through those forests with no one to see or hear me, pondering about God and his plan for me. Also, thinking about the few people who believed in me. Smelling the trees on the logging trucks. I will never forget that scent. The friendly wave and toot of the horn from the truck drivers always made my day.

Knowing I was a little nuts but believing every morning looking up at the clouds that my mother, grandmother, and Gary were sitting on a cloud looking down on me. Saint Christopher, this six-foot dude with a goatee, was on my left, keeping me straight. Saint Francis, with his beer belly, was on my right, directing all the animals that I met to come up and put their heads on my shoulder.

Did I expect to be a celebrity or a hero? No, I was not doing this for the glory or the hoopla! I realize that I am the same person, hopefully a good person who has made mistakes like everybody else in life. Did my kids love me more? Did my friends respect me more? Did associates look at me differently?

Regardless of the person I was, kindness cost nothing. Whatever your beliefs, kindness is always something you can give without any compensation.

My walk was a mission to bring attention to the wounded warriors. Most people cannot comprehend what these warriors have gone through. Imagine waking up each morning seeing and knowing that a part of your body is missing. Always in constant pain, these warriors' sacrifices for the love of their country have no dollar amount.

Unfortunately, how many people, politicians and others, really have little or no respect for our country or our flag?

When I was a midshipman at the United States Merchant Marine Academy, we had colors every morning, with the band playing the national anthem. I was in charge of our dog mascot at colors. Guess what kind of dog. It was a Saint Bernard! At attention, saluting that flag, knowing what our flag represented would send chills up my spine. To this day, every time I hear "The Star-Spangled Banner," I still get chills up my spine. I feel very sad when people during the playing of our anthem disrespect it. They have the right to disrespect it and do whatever, but if they could have seen and talked to the wounded warriors I met on my journey, I believe they would have second thoughts about their actions.

It's easy to criticize our country, but it takes a belief in what's good to support our country. On my walk, I thought about the troops on the ships the night before D-Day, what was going through their minds, knowing they were probably going to die the next morning. The family and friends they would never see again. My only regret about dying is I will not be able to hug my children. Always, I love hugging them and letting them know how much I love them.

I can't explain people's reaction when they see me wearing my shirt that states "I Walked from Tampa to the Bronx." Some ignore me, and others ask, "Did you really do it?" Most of them have no clue about the hardships of my walk. My reaction to myself is, look into my soul, look into my heart, and feel what kindness each one of us is capable of.

I recently gave a presentation to a veterans' group in the community where I am currently living. I played some of my actual audio journal entries. It was the first time I'd heard them since my walk concluded. At the end, there wasn't a dry eye in the place! The audience gave me a standing ovation. In my heart I was hoping every wounded warrior would know that ovation was for them.

Am I any different today? No, but I am more proud of knowing who I am. I love my country. I have a profoundly deep respect for our wounded warriors and a sadness for people who don't take the time to realize that kindness costs nothing!

# *Epilogue*

Below is a reprint of the *Congressional Record* of June 16, 2015, relating Representative David W. Jolly's speech.

*Mr. Speaker, I rise today to recognize a man who has literally walked the Walk in support of our Nation's wounded warriors.*

*Mr. Speaker, 65-year-old Richard Albero, a former naval officer and math teacher from Dunedin, Florida, recently completed an 86-day, 1,150-mile Walk from home plate at Steinbrenner Field in Tampa during a spring training game to home plate at Yankee Stadium in New York City. He did so to honor his fallen nephew. Richard's nephew, Gary, worked at the World Trade Center and lost his life in the 9/11 attacks.*

*In addition to honoring his nephew, Richard also chose to do something very special. He walked to raise money for the Wounded Warrior Project. His goal was to raise $25,000.*

*During Richard's trek up the East Coast, which began on March 2, he went through six pairs of shoes. He suffered blisters on his feet and traveled over countless hills and endured the many elements, yet Richard never gave up.*

*Very recently, just a few weeks ago, he completed his Walk, arriving at Yankee Stadium to a cheering crowd.*

*Along the way, Richard blew past his goal for raising money and raised $55,000 for the Wounded Warrior Project.*

*Mr. Speaker, Richard's nephew would be most proud and the Members of this body should be most proud as well as we reflect on and remember those who lost their lives and those who pay tribute to them today, those like Richard Albero.*

*May God bless Mr. Albero. May God bless our men and women in uniform who protect us each and every day. And may God bless these United States.*

On the plane home to Florida, I remember watching the small TV monitor on the back of the seat tracking my flight. It showed my plane with its flight pattern over the East Coast. I looked at all the eastern states and said, "Holy cow, did I really walk all that way?" It seemed so surreal to me. I just started to laugh. The person next to me looked at me like I was crazy.

Immediately upon returning to Dunedin, Florida, I put my house up for sale. I sold it a short time later. True to my soul, I purchased a three-acre minifarm in Ocala, Florida. I volunteer as head chef one day a week at a local food pantry. It was strange traveling on roads I had walked just a short time earlier.

I purchased two Sicilian donkeys and named them Angelina and Henrietta. I started to train them to be therapy donkeys. I envisioned inviting wounded warriors to my farm to ride the donkeys, swim, and have a barbecue gathering.

Unfortunately, many factors sabotaged me in this endeavor. My next-door neighbor told me he was worried about having wounded warriors at my house. He said they might go off. He had children to be concerned about. I wonder if he felt the same way when they were fighting for his family's freedom in Iraq.

I was in love with Ocala's countryside and its beauty, but I had no real support. I felt very isolated. I decided to make a move farther south and be closer to family. I do not regret trying this adventure. I knew it was a worthwhile quest. I was still tired from my walk. Also, I found a very nice sanctuary for my donkeys. I will always miss going out to the donkey pasture. Seeing me coming out to the stable, the donkeys would start to bray and looked for my homemade donkey biscuits. Decision made, I sold my home in Ocala.

People who meet me and know about my adventures usually ask me, "What's next?" My response with a smile is "We'll see." Sometimes I just want to get on a plane and go to Syria and help those poor war-stricken children be a little more comfortable and safe. Unfortunately, I am too old and underqualified to accomplish that. Sometimes I envision myself as a volunteer for Doctors without Borders.

At the moment I spend my Mondays visiting a local hospital in Bradenton, Florida, with my therapy Saint Bernard dog Mia. It is so rewarding watching the happiness and joy she brings the patients, nurses, doctors, and other personnel. Tuesdays, Mia and I visit a nursing home in Sarasota. It's sad in many ways seeing these poor souls completing their final journeys. I always say a prayer for them and hope Mia's and my visits with them bring some joy to their lives. Hopefully these visits take their minds off their discomfort and loneliness. Wednesdays, it's a soup kitchen in Bradenton. Not the head chef, but a good lesson in humility volunteering as a helping hand. The rest of the week, I just try to be kind and wait for God to tap me on the shoulder for my next journey.

Finally, I hope you found some form of comfort reading my book. If nothing else, if you remember *kindness costs nothing* and *the family is everything*, then this was a worthwhile endeavor.

Thank you and God bless!

# About the Author

Richard John Albero is a former naval officer, high school and college teacher, and a single parent of three children. Retired, he lives in Florida with two St. Bernard dogs. He spends most of his time with his St. Bernard therapy dog, Mia, visiting nursing homes and hospitals. Albero works on improving his cooking, poker, and canasta skills.